D#

P9-CKX-964

7-2494

The Hiker's Guide
to NEW MEXICO

by
Laurence Parent

FALCON PRESS

Helena, Montana

ACKNOWLEDGMENTS

Many people contributed to this book, more than can be listed here.

Special thanks goes to my wife, Patricia, for accompanying me on hikes when her busy schedule allowed and, even more, for suffering my long absences from home.

Friends and family offered me their hospitality during the extensive travels necessary for this book. My parents, Hiram and Annette; my sister and her husband, Anne and Pat Fischer; David and Debbie Dozier; John and Adamina Morlock; Jack Shlachter; Cathy Bowman; and Nancy Wizner all put me up for the night. I hope that they didn't get too tired of the sight of me camping out in their guest rooms.

Pat Fischer was an excellent companion on a number of hikes. After a long spell of solitary hikes, Teresa Sanders and Tonya Hays were welcome companions on the next-to-last hike done for this book.

Steve and Peg Fleming deserve thanks for patiently posing for photos. The REI store in Albuquerque graciously allowed me to use their extensive map collection. Many Forest Service, Park Service, and BLM personnel endured numerous questions. Particularly helpful were Ron Henderson of the Gila National Forest and Phil Dano of the Cibola National Forest. I would also like to thank Bill Blackard of the BLM and Cindy Ott-Jones of the El Malpais National Monument.

Falcon Press is continually expanding its list of recreational guidebooks using the same general format as this book. All books include detailed descriptions, accurate maps, and all information necessary for enjoyable trips. You can order extra copies of this book and get information and prices for other Falcon books by writing Falcon Press, P.O. Box 1718, Helena, MT 59624. Also, please ask for a free copy of our current catalog listing all Falcon Press books.

Falcon Press Publishing Co., Inc., P.O. Box 1718, Helena, MT 59624

All text, maps, and photos by the author. Photos by the author except as noted.
Cover Photo: Laurence Parent, White Sands National Monument.

Library of Congress Cataloging-in-Publication Data

Parent, Laurence.
  The hiker's guide to New Mexico / Laurence Parent.
     p.   cm.
  Reprint. Previously published: c1991.
  "A Falcon guide."—P. 4 of cover
  ISBN 1-56044-064-3 : $9.95
  1. Hiking—New Mexico—Guidebooks. 2. New Mexico—Guidebooks.
  I. Title.
GV199.42.N6P37   1993   91-70766
796.5'1'09789—dc20   CIP

 Text pages printed on recycled paper.

CONTENTS

LOCATION OF HIKES

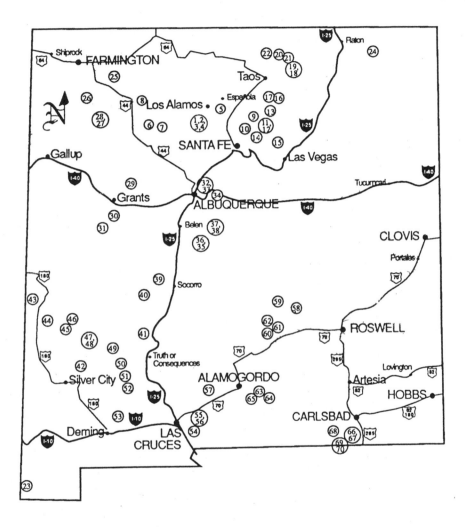

The New Mexico backcountry is one of uncommon and diverse beauty. Douglas fir on the Sandia Crest in the Sandia Mountains.

HIKING IN NEW MEXICO, AN INTRODUCTION

New Mexico is a diverse state, with almost any kind of terrain and climate imaginable. One day you can be sweltering in the desert backcountry of Carlsbad Caverns National Park, the next you can be shivering at an alpine lake as snow flurries shroud the peaks above. The ancient ruins of Bandelier National Monument lie in stark contrast to the government labs in adjacent Los Alamos. The skyscrapers of Albuquerque rise into the sky only sixty miles south of Santa Fe's 350-year-old Palace of the Governors. The lush spruce forests of the Sangre de Cristo Mountains seem worlds away from the sere desert along the Jornada del Muerto, the Journey of Death.

New Mexico's great range of elevations, from about 3,000 feet to over 13,000 feet, creates a wide variety of climates, vegetation, and terrain. People unfamiliar with the state often believe that most of New Mexico is little more than desert. Many are surprised to find that over a quarter of the state is forested. In northern New Mexico, southern extensions of the Rocky Mountains boast peaks higher than 13,000 feet. Many other mountain ranges pepper the rest of the state, most with elevations of 10,000 feet or higher.

Elevation largely controls climate in New Mexico. The state's broad range gives rise to six life zones, from the Lower Sonoran, with its creosote, cacti, and other desert plants, to the Alpine Zone, with its tundra. The mountains attract most of the rainfall, with some receiving forty inches of rain and snow per year. In contrast, some desert areas receive as little as eight inches per year. Likewise, temperatures vary widely, with record extremes of minus-50 degrees to 116 degrees Fahrenheit. The wide variation in elevation and climate provide year-round hiking opportunities.

Most of the hikes in this guide lie in mountain areas because of their scenic beauty and the high concentrations of public land. Also, most developed trails lie in the mountains.

A guidebook of manageable size can only include a fraction of the possible hikes in a state the size of New Mexico. One thousand miles of trail stretch across the Santa Fe National Forest alone. However, I've tried to include a cross section of hikes from all parts of the state. I've included popular hikes, such as the La Luz Trail, but also many obscure hikes, such as Cooks Peak. All of the hikes lie on public land, especially the national forests and national parks. The vast majority of trailheads are accessible by any type of vehicle; only a few require high clearance or four-wheel-drive.

If you are a beginning hiker, don't let the length of some of these hikes intimidate you. Don't restrict yourself to only the short ones. Most of the long hikes are very beautiful and rewarding even if you only go a half mile down the trail.

Although the hikes in this guide may keep you busy for years, many of the hikes suggest additional nearby routes or extensions of the described hike. Don't be afraid to try them. This book serves best as an introduction to many of the most beautiful backcountry areas of New Mexico.

Using the guide

The Hiker's Guide to New Mexico describes seventy hikes scattered widely across the state. The map at the start of this book indicates their locations. Several categories of information describe each hike. The general description gives a brief one-sentence description of the hike, along with its degree of difficulty. The general location gives the hike's location in regard to the closest significant town or park. The length gives the approximate length of the hike as a round trip; that is, the distance from the trailhead to the destination and back to the trailhead. The elevation lists the highest and lowest points reached on the hike. The map category suggests maps to use for the hike. The best season gives the best time of year, weatherwise, for the hike. Water availability lists sites on the hike where water can be found. Special attractions describe some of the high points of the hike. Permit information is listed if permits are required to enter or camp in an area.

Finding the trailhead provides detailed directions for locating the start of each hike. The hike provides a detailed description of the hike itself, usually with some introductory information about the area.

Detailed maps accompany each hike. The map information was taken from USGS topo maps, national forest maps, BLM maps, and national park maps. Use the guidebook's maps in conjunction with the government maps.

General description

The general description provides three categories of information. Besides giving a brief summary of the hike, it assigns the hike its degree of difficulty and suggests the amount of time required for the hike.

Assessing a hike's difficulty is very subjective. Not only do the elevation, elevation change, and length play a role, but trail condition, weather, and physical condition of the hiker are important. I probably rated some of the first hikes that I did for this book as more difficult than they are and some of the last hikes, when I was in much better physical condition, as easier than they really are. However, even my subjective ratings will give some idea of difficulty. To me, elevation gain was the most significant variable in establishing levels of difficulty.

In general, if a hike gains less than 1,000 feet and is less than eight miles round trip, I usually rated it as easy. Within each category there are many degrees of difficulty, of course. Obviously a two-mile hike gaining two hundred feet is going to be much easier than an eight-mile hike gaining 900 feet.

Moderate hikes, probably the most common in this book, usually gain somewhere between 1,000 and 2,000 feet and run longer than eight miles. The strenuous hikes usually gain over 2,000 feet and are fairly long. Poor trails, excessive heat, high elevations with thin air, cross-country travel, and other factors may result in a more difficult designation than would otherwise seem to be the case.

Carrying a heavy backpack can make even an "easy" day hike fairly strenuous. All the designations assume snow-free trails. Early and late season hikes in the high mountains will be considerably more difficult if you are having to trudge through snow drifts.

The hiking speed of different people varies considerably. A hike is loosely classified as a day hike if most reasonably fit people can easily complete it in one day or less. Likewise, two- or three-day hikes can be easily done by most reasonably fit people in two or three days. Many of the day hikes, although easily done in one day, have attractions that make them worthy of longer, relaxed stays. A few of the day hikes, particularly in some of the National Park Service areas, must be done in a day because overnight camping is not allowed.

Length

The length specified in each description is listed as a round-trip distance from the trailhead to the end of the route and back. As mentioned in the individual hike descriptions, some of the hikes work well with car shuttles. Setting up such shuttles with two cars can halve the round trip mileage of some of the hikes. Alternatively, someone can pick up your group at a set time at the end of the route. Another method involves splitting the group, dropping off the first half at one end, and parking the car and starting the other half from the other end of the hike. When the two groups meet in the middle, they exchange car keys, allowing the first group to later pick up the second. All hike mileages assume, however, that you are unable to arrange a shuttle.

Hike lengths have been estimated as closely as possible using topographic maps and government measurements. However, the different sources do not always agree, so the final figure is sometimes the author's best estimate.

Elevation

Elevation is generally the most important factor in determining a hike's difficulty. The two numbers listed are the highest and lowest points reached on the hike. Often, but not always, the trailhead lies at the low point and the end lies at the highest point. With canyon hikes, the numbers are sometimes reversed. Most of the hikes have a fairly steady climb going out and a fairly steady downhill coming back. Some of the hikes have several ups and downs on the way, requiring more elevation gain and effort. The Stone Lions, Hike 3, is a notable example. The detailed hike descriptions indicate such trails.

Absolute elevation affects difficulty, also. New Mexico is very high state, with its lowest point lying at almost 3,000 feet. At high elevations, lower atmospheric pressure creates "thin air." The thin air requires higher breathing rates and more effort to pull enough oxygen into lungs. Since most of these hikes lie in the mountains, many lie at elevations of 8,000 feet or more. A good number of the hikes in the northern part of the state climb as high as 11,000, 12,000, or 13,000 feet. Most people will at least partially acclimate to the thin air after a few days. Hikers coming from low elevation areas, such as neighboring Texas, may want to do easy hikes at moderate altitudes for the first couple of days.

Maps

The maps in this guide are as accurate and current as possible. When used in conjunction with the description and the maps listed in each hike's heading, you should have little trouble following the route.

Generally, up to three types of maps are listed. The national forest maps usually show the trails, but, because of their small scale, rarely give enough detail to be especially helpful. However, they are very useful for locating forest roads, trailheads, and campgrounds. They are generally more current than the USGS topographic maps and usually show the level of improvement of the forest roads. The National Park Service often has maps or brochures showing the trails. They vary in their usefulness.

USGS topographic quadrangles are generally the most detailed and accurate maps available of natural features. With practice you can visualize peaks, canyons, cliffs, and many other features. With a little experience, a topographic map, and a compass, you should never become lost. Topographic maps are particularly useful for little-used trails and off-trail travel. Unfortunately, many of the quadrangles, particularly in the New Mexico hinterlands, are way out of date and do not show current manmade features such as roads and trails. However, they are still useful for their topographic information.

In recent years, government agencies have drawn up maps of many of the state's wilderness areas. All are set on topographic maps, although sometimes at a smaller scale than the USGS maps. So you not only get topographic information, the roads and trails are usually fairly current. When available for a given hike, the wilderness maps are probably adequate for all but off-trail hikes. The maps are a good compromise and cheaper to buy and easier to carry than a forest map and several USGS quads.

Snow can fall at any time of the year in the New Mexico backcountry, as the picture of Shiprock illustrates.

The wilderness and forest maps are usually available at ranger stations and at many outdoor shops in the larger cities. Currently most cost $2 each, but some, on plastic stock, are $4 or a little more. National Park Service and BLM maps and brochures are usually available at no or small cost at the park visitor centers.

USGS quads can usually be found at outdoor shops or ordered directly from USGS. To order, list the state, the number desired of each map, the exact map name as listed in the hike heading, and the scale. Send your order to the U.S. Geological Survey, ESIC-Denver, 169 Federal Building, 1961 Stout Street, Denver, CO 80294, (303) 844-4169. Call before sending your order to determine current prices.

MAP LEGEND

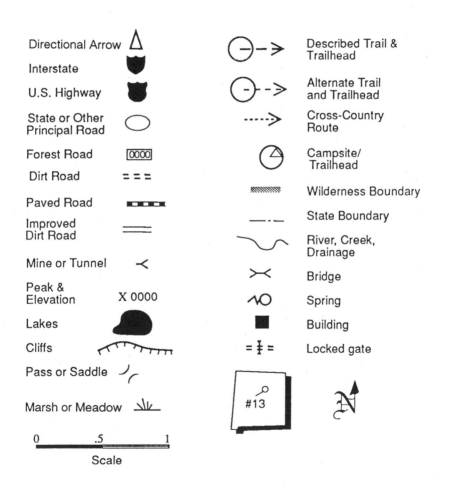

Directional Arrow

Interstate

U.S. Highway

State or Other Principal Road

Forest Road

Dirt Road

Paved Road

Improved Dirt Road

Mine or Tunnel

Peak & Elevation   X 0000

Lakes

Cliffs

Pass or Saddle

Marsh or Meadow

0   .5   1

Scale

Described Trail & Trailhead

Alternate Trail and Trailhead

Cross-Country Route

Campsite/ Trailhead

Wilderness Boundary

State Boundary

River, Creek, Drainage

Bridge

Spring

Building

Locked gate

#13

Best Season

The season specified for a hike is the optimum or ideal season. For instance, most of the mountain hikes are covered with snow much of the year. The months specified are those in which little or no snowpack covers the trail in normal years. The areas are not closed during winter months; however experience with skis or snowshoes and winter travel is required. Several of the hikes, as noted in the descriptions, are marked for use as cross-country ski trails in winter.

The months specified are average; heavy spring snows can sometimes cover trails at the highest elevations well into summer and early winters can close trails ahead of time. Conversely, dry winters can greatly extend the optimum hiking season. At the highest elevations, especially in northern New Mexico, snow flurries can come even in the middle of summer, so be prepared. Local Forest Service ranger stations can tell you trail conditions for early or late season hikes.

The low elevation and desert hikes are usually hikable year round. However, summers can be very hot, especially at places like Carlsbad Caverns and White Sands. Snow falls occasionally at the low elevations, but usually melts off within a day or two. Spring can be dry and windy, making desert hikes unpleasant at times. Fall is probably the premier time for low elevation hikes. Always check weather forecasts before starting your hike.

Water availability

Sources of water are listed if they are known to usually be reliable. Any water obtained on a hike should be purified before use. Be sure to check with a ranger station about the status of water sources before depending on them. Droughts, livestock and wildlife use, and other factors can change their status.

Permit

Permits are not usually required for wilderness or backcountry entry in New Mexico. Several of the National Park Service areas allow only day use on certain trails. Generally all National Park Service areas require you to obtain a free permit for overnight trips.

Finding the trailhead

This section provides detailed directions to the trailheads. With a current state highway map, you can easily locate the starting point from the directions. In general, the nearest significant town was used as the starting point.

One warning: be sure to get a current highway map. For unfathomable bureaucratic reasons, the state highway department has changed the numbers on most of New Mexico's highways during the last few years. Thus, state highways shown on all but the most current U.S. Forest Service, National Park Service, USGS, and highway maps will be numbered incorrectly. This guide uses the new numbers throughout.

Driving distances were measured with a car odometer. Realize that different cars will vary slightly in their measurements. Even the same car will read slightly differently driving up a dirt road versus down a dirt road. So be sure to keep an eye open for the specific signs, junctions, and landmarks mentioned in the directions.

Vandals damage many trail signs; this one is in the Pecos Wilderness.

Most of this guide's hikes were selected to have trailheads that could be reached by a sedan. A few, as noted, require high clearance and, except in wet or snowy weather, none require a four-wheel drive. Rain or snow can temporarily make some roads impassable. Before venturing onto unimproved forest roads, you should check with the local ranger station. On less-travelled back roads, you should carry basic emergency equipment, such as a shovel, chains, water, a spare tire, a jack, blankets, and some extra food and clothing. Make sure that your vehicle is in good operating condition with a full tank of gas.

Theft and vandalism occasionally occurs at trailheads. The local ranger station or sheriff's office can tell you of any recent problems. Try not to leave valuables in the car at all; if you must, lock them out of sight in the trunk. If I have enough room in the trunk, I usually put everything in to give the car an overall empty appearance. In my many years of parking and hiking at remote trailheads, I have never had my vehicle disturbed.

The hike

All of the hikes selected for this guide can be easily done by people in good physical condition. A little scrambling may be necessary in a few, but none require any rock climbing skills. A few of the hikes, as noted in their descriptions, travel across country or on very faint trails. You should have an experienced hiker, along with a compass and USGS quad, with your group before doing those hikes.

The trails are often marked with rock cairns or blazes. Most of the time, the trail are very obvious and easy to follow, but the marks help when the trails are little-used and faint. Cairns are piles of rock built along the route. Tree blazes are i-shaped carvings on trees, usually at shoulder or head height. Blazes can be especially useful when a forest trail is obscured by snow. Be sure not to add your own blazes or cairns; it can confuse the route. Leave such markings to the official trail workers.

Possible campsites are often suggested in the descriptions. Many others are usually available. Except for a few of the National Park Service areas, few restrictions usually exist in selecting a campsite, provided that it is well away from the trail or any water source.

After reading the descriptions, pick the hike that appeals most. Go only as far as ability and desire allow. There's no obligation to complete any hike. Remember, you are out hiking to enjoy yourself, not to prove anything.

Hiking with children

Don't automatically hunt for the baby sitter the next time that you want to go hiking. Kids of almost any age will enjoy a hiking trip if they aren't pushed beyond their ability.

The following hikes should entice children. A few may be difficult if hiked in their entirety, but most are easy and all are interesting even if only hiked a short distance.

You can't lose taking children of any age to White Sands (Hike 57). Of course you may spend the next two days getting the sand out of everything. In summer, the swarms of ladybugs that descend on the crest of Capulin Volcano (Hike 24) will delight children of all ages.

The ladders, caves, and stream on the easy hike to Ceremonial Cave (Hike 2) are great for older children. The cliffs and long ladders that create much of its appeal necessitate close supervision. The Gila Cliff Dwellings (Hike 47) is another easy hike through caves and Indian ruins.

Some good hikes along streams include two in the Pecos Wilderness (Hikes 13 and 14), Whitewater Creek (Hike 44), the Mimbres River (Hike 49), and Argentina Canyon (Hike 62). Children will love the hike along the east fork of the Jemez River (Hike 7)—you have to wade.

Sitting Bull Falls (Hike 68) is a sure winner. The water is much warmer than most of the high mountain streams and invites wading and swimming. However, unless your kids are older and very responsible, don't take them to the top of the falls; stay at the stream below the falls.

WILDERNESS ETHICS

A few simple rules and courtesies will help in both preserving the wilderness environment and allowing others to enjoy their outdoor experience. Every hiker has at least a slight impact on the land and other visitors. Your goal should be to minimize that impact. Some of the rules and suggestions may seen overly restrictive and confining, but with increasing use of shrinking wild areas, such rules have become more necessary. All can be followed with little inconvenience and will contribute to a better outdoors experience for you and others.

Camping

Camp at least 100 yards away from water sources. The vegetation at creeks, lakes, and springs is often the most fragile. Camping well away prevents trampling and destruction of the plant life. Destruction of vegetation usually leads to erosion and muddying of water sources. Additionally, camping 100 yards away limits runoff of wash water, food scraps, and human waste. An advantage to dry camps is that they are usually warmer and have less insects. Additionally, in desert areas, a spring may be the only water source for miles. If you camp too close, you may keep wildlife from reaching water.

Pick a level site that won't require modification to be usable. Don't destroy vegetation in setting up camp. The ideal camp is probably on a bare forest floor carpeted with pine needles. Don't trench around the tent site. Pick a spot with good natural drainage. If possible pick a site that has already been used so that you won't trample another. If you remove rock, sticks, or other debris, replace them when you depart. You want to leave no trace of your passage.

Don't pitch your tent right next to someone else's camp. Remember, they are probably out here to get away from people, too. Likewise, set up camp out of sight of trails and avoid creating excessive noise.

If backcountry toilets are available, use them. Otherwise, dig a six to eight-inch-deep hole as far away from water, campsites, and trails as possible and bury human wastes. At that depth, it will quickly decompose. If weather and forest conditions allow, carefully burn toilet paper; otherwise carry it out with you. Fish entrails should be burned or buried. Don't dispose of them in the water.

Carry out all of your trash that hasn't been burned. Remember that those foil freeze-dried food packages won't burn completely. Animals will dig up any garbage that you bury. Improve the area for future visitors and take out trash that others have left behind.

Campfires leave permanent scars. If you must build one, do it on bare soil without a fire ring. Use only dead and fallen wood. Put it out thoroughly with water and never leave it unattended. Buried fires can sometimes escape from under the soil. Don't start a fire on dry or windy days. The forests of New Mexico are notoriously dry in late spring and early summer before the rainy season. The national forests often limit the use of fires during this time. Be sure to honor the restrictions.

Except in an emergency, don't use campfires in areas near timberline. Trees grow very slowly in the harsh conditions at high elevations, making firewood

Backpackers should camp at least 100 yards from any water source. Lake Katherine, at the foot of Santa Fe Baldy

very limited. Likewise, don't use fires in any other areas, such as deserts, where wood is obviously scarce. For cooking purposes, backpacking stoves are much easier, quicker, and more efficient.

Carry an extra empty gallon jug or wash basin to use for washing yourself or cooking utensils. Use the jug to carry water and wash well away from the water source to keep soap and other pollutants from flowing into the water.

The trail

Don't shortcut switchbacks on the trail. Switchbacks were built to ease the grade on climbs and to limit erosion. Shortcutting, although it may be shorter, usually takes more effort and unquestionably creates additional erosion.

Always give horses and other pack animals the right of way. Stand well away from the trail and make no sudden movements or noises that could spook the animals.

If you smoke, stop in a safe spot and make sure that cigarettes and matches are dead out before proceeding. Be sure to take your butts with you. Don't smoke in windy and dry conditions.

Motorized and mechanized vehicles, including mountain bikes, are prohibited from all wilderness and most national park trails. Other areas may also have restrictions.

Don't do anything to disturb the natural environment. Don't cut live trees or plants. Resist the temptation to pick wildflowers. Don't blaze trees, carve initials on aspens, build bridges, or add improvements to campsites. Don't remove any Indian relics or other historic items. All historic items are protected by law on government lands.

If you take your dog, please be courteous. Dogs will often annoy other hikers seeking a wilderness experience. Leash him if other hikers are around. Keep him away from water sources to avoid possible pollution. Keep him from disturbing wildlife. Keep him quiet, especially at night. In general, it's probably best to leave your pet at home.

National Parks

Rules in National Park Service areas are generally more restrictive than in other government lands. Some park areas do not permit back country camping. Others require campsites to be located in specific areas. All require that free overnight permits be obtained. Dogs are not allowed on trails, nor may any plants, rocks, or other items be removed. Use of campfires is usually more restricted. Because of dry conditions and lack of wood, Carlsbad Caverns prohibits the use of campfires altogether. Hunting is prohibited in park areas, but fishing is usually permitted with appropriate state licenses.

Other restrictions may apply at certain areas. Local ranger stations and signs at trailheads can inform you of any requirements.

SAFETY

With common sense and good judgment, few mishaps should occur. Don't push yourself or companions beyond physical ability. Be aware of changing weather. Know basic first aid techniques.

The following list elaborates on some of the potential hazards that you may encounter on your hikes. Don't let the list scare you. I've been hiking for over twenty years without any serious mishap. The few incidents that have occurred usually were due to carelessness on my part: carrying too little water, not using sunscreen, pushing beyond my limits, etc.

Weather

More problems and emergencies in the outdoors are probably related to weather than any other other factor. Even in the hot desert areas, sudden thunderstorms in late summer can drench you, and at the least, make you uncomfortably cool. In the high mountains, temperatures can plummet in storms. When combined with wet clothes or lack of shelter, a life threatening situation can develop.

It's easy to prepare for most weather problems. Always take extra, warm clothes, especially on extended hikes. Wool and some synthetics still retain some insulating capability when wet; cotton is worthless. Rain gear is essential, especially on hikes in the higher mountains in late summer. Carry a reliable tent on the longer hikes. Hole up and wait for the bad weather to pass, rather than attempting a long hike out. Most storms in New Mexico, especially in summer, are of short duration.

Hypothermia develops when the body's temperature falls. New Mexico is usually thought of as a desert state, but many of these hikes are in high mountain areas where hypothermia is a risk. If conditions turn wet and cold and a member of your party begins to slur speech, shiver constantly, or becomes clumsy, sleepy, or unreasonable, it is wise to assume hypothermia is the cause and immediately get the hiker into shelter and out of wet clothes. Give the victim warm liquids to drink and get him into a sleeping bag with one or more people. Skin-to-skin contact conducts body heat to the victim most effectively. This isn't a time for modesty; you may save the victim's life.

At the other extreme, heat can cause problems, particularly in summer in the low elevation areas of southern New Mexico. On hot-weather hikes, carry and drink adequate water. For long hikes in hot weather, plan to carry at least a gallon of water per person per day. Hikes in New Mexico can be quite hot even as high as 7,000 feet or more in May and June, before the summer rains begin. If you do desert hikes in summer, try to get a very early start to avoid the worst of the heat. Don't push as hard; take frequent breaks.

With heat exhaustion, the skin is still moist and sweaty, but the victim may feel weak, dizzy, nauseated, or have muscle cramps. Find a cool shady place to rest and feed him plenty of liquids and a few crackers or other source of salt. After the victim feels better, keep him drinking plenty of liquids and limit physical activity. Hike out during a cooler time of day. The condition usually isn't serious, but take the hiker to a doctor as soon as possible.

Thunderstorms are a constant danger in the New Mexico mountains. A storm builds up over the Black Range.

Heatstroke is less common, but can develop with prolonged exposure to very hot conditions. The body's temperature regulation system stops functioning, resulting in a rapid rise in body temperature. The skin is hot, flushed, and bone-dry. Confusion and unconsciousness can quickly follow. The situation is life-threatening. Immediately get the victim into the coolest available place. Remove excess clothes and dampen skin and remaining clothes with water. Fan the victim for additional cooling. If a cool stream or pond is nearby, consider immersing the victim. You must get the body temperature down quickly. Seek medical help immediately.

Lightning poses another threat. New Mexico has the notorious distinction of having the highest per capita number of lightning deaths in the country. When thunderstorms develop, seek lower ground. Stay off ridges and peaks and away from lone trees, lakes, and open areas. Lightning makes high areas above timberline especially hazardous. Plan to start your hikes early to reach high peaks and ridges by lunch time and head down promptly. The most common thunderstorms in New Mexico develop in the afternoons of late summer. If you get caught in a lightning storm, seek shelter in a low-lying grove of small equal-sized trees if possible. Put down your metal-framed packs, tripods, and metal tent poles well away from you.

Heavy rains can also cause flooding. Stay out of narrow canyons boxed in by cliffs during heavy rains. Even though you may be in sunshine, watch the weather upstream from you. Camp well above and away from streams and rivers. Never camp in that tempting sandy site in the bottom of a dry desert wash. Storms upstream from you can send water sweeping down desert washes with unbelievable fury.

Physical preparation

Good physical condition will not only make your trip safer, but much more pleasant. Don't push yourself too hard, especially at high altitudes. If you have been sedentary for a long time, consider getting a physical exam before starting hiking. Ease into hiking; start with the easy hikes and graduate to more difficult ones. Don't push your party any harder or faster than the weakest member feels comfortable with. Know your limits. When you get tired, rest or turn back. Remember, you are out here to have fun.

Be mentally prepared. Read this guidebook and the specific hike description. Study maps and other books on the area. Every effort has been made to create a guide book that is as accurate and current as possible, but a few errors may still creep in. Additionally, roads and trails change. Signs can disappear, springs can dry up, roads can wash out, and trails can be rerouted. Talk to rangers about current road and trail conditions and water sources. Check the weather forecast. Find out the abilities and desires of your hiking companions before hitting the trail.

Altitude

Many of New Mexico's mountains are relatively high. People coming from low elevations, especially out of state, may have some trouble at altitudes above 8000 feet. Until you acclimate, you may suffer from shortness of breath and tire more easily. A few hikers may develop headaches, nausea, fatigue, or other mild symptoms such as swelling of the face, hands, ankles, or other body areas at the highest altitudes. Mild symptoms shouldn't change your plans. Rest for a day or two to acclimate. Retreating a thousand feet or so will often clear up any symptoms. New Mexico residents should have less trouble than most, since over half of the people in the state already live at 5,000 feet or higher. Spending several days at moderate altitude before climbing high will often prevent any problems.

New Mexico's mountains are not high enough to cause the serious symptoms of altitude sickness, such as pulmonary edema (fluid collecting in the lungs) or cerebral edema (fluid accumulating in the brain), except in very rare cases. Should these symptoms develop, immediately get the victim to lower elevations and medical attention.

Companions

Pick your companions wisely. Consider their experience and physical and mental fitness. Try to form groups of relatively similar physical ability. Pick a leader, especially on long trips or with large groups. Ideally, have at least one experienced hiker with the group.

Too large a group is unwieldy and diminishes the wilderness experience for yourself and others. An ideal size is probably four. In case of injury, one can stay with the victim, while the other two can hike out for help. No one is left alone. Leave your travel plans with friends so that they can send help if you do not appear. Allow plenty of time for your trip; trips often run later than expected.

Never hike alone, especially cross-country or on little-traveled routes. That said, I must confess that I did most of the hikes in this guide alone. However, I religiously informed family or friends of my travel plans on a daily basis and did not deviate from them. Upon returning from a hike I immediately called to let them know that I was back. Never forget to check in at the end of your hike. Nothing will aggravate rescuers more than to find that you were at the local bar relaxing with a beer while they were stumbling around in the rain and dark looking for you.

The only time that I did not worry about informing friends of my travel plans was when I did popular hikes on summer weekends. Plenty of other people were on the trail if a mishap occurred.

Water

Unfortunately, with the heavy use that many backcountry areas are receiving, all water sources should be purified before use. Most hikers will not get sick if the water is obtained directly from springs or from streams near their source in little-used areas. However, it is best to play it safe and always treat your water. Boiling vigorously for ten minutes (more at higher altitudes) is a reliable method, but slow and consumes a lot fuel.

Mechanical filtration units are available at most outdoors shops. Filters with a very small pore size strain out bacteria, viruses, cysts, and other microorganisms. Their ability to filter out the smallest organisms, such as viruses, varies from model to model. For very contaminated water, filtration should probably be used in conjunction with chemical treatment.

Chemical treatment is probably the easiest method. Chlorination is the method used by most municipal water systems, but the use of hyperiodide tablets is probably safer and more reliable for backpackers. They can be purchased at any outdoors store. Follow the directions carefully. Cold or cloudy water requires more chemical use or longer treatment times.

The cleaner that your water is from the start, the better. Get your water from springs or upstream from trails and camps if possible. For day hikes, it is usually easiest just to carry sufficient water for the day.

Stream crossings

Crossing all but the smallest of streams poses several hazards. Except in flood stage, few of the streams along the trails in this guide are big enough to pose much of a risk of to hikers. However, do not underestimate the power of fast flowing rivers, such as the Rio Grande, Pecos, Gila, or smaller streams in flood. Avoid crossing high volume waterways when possible. If you must cross them, try to find rocks or logs to use, although they may be slippery. Or try to find a broad, slow moving shallow stretch for your ford. Undo the waist strap on your backpack for quick removal if necessary. Use a stout walking stick for stability.

Since the vast majority of the streams in New Mexico are too small to sweep you away, the biggest risk probably lies in jumping from rock to rock or crossing on logs to avoid wet feet. Often the rocks or logs are unstable or slippery, making falls possible. A heavy pack makes such crossings even more tricky. While such a fall might not be life threatening, a twisted ankle or broken leg would present problems. Use extra care and assist each other across streams.

Insects

Insects present more of a nuisance than threat in New Mexico. Summer is the most likely time for problems. Moquitoes will hatch after heavy summer rains, even in desert regions. In general, mosquitoes are more of a problem in the high, lush mountains than in the desert. A repellant containing DEET in high percentages will discourage mosquitoes and gnats from bothering you. Camp well away from streams, marshes, and other wet areas. Good mosquito netting on your tent will allow a pleasant night's sleep. I have camped many a time in dry areas without a tent or netting with no problems at all.

Ticks create only a minor problem in New Mexico. However, they do carry serious diseases, such as Rocky Mountain spotted fever and Lyme disease, so be aware of them. Use insect repellant, wear clothing that fits snugly around the waist, ankles, and wrists, and check yourself and pets every night. If a tick attaches, remove it promptly. Use tweezers and avoid squeezing the tick as you pull it out. Do not leave the head embedded and do not handle the tick. Apply antiseptic to the bite and wash thoroughly. Ticks are probably most common in livestock areas. If you develop any sickness within two or three weeks of the bite, see a doctor.

One of the pleasures of growing up in New Mexico was its paucity of nuisance insects. In all of my hiking and camping, I have only had one tick on my body. I got it after sitting for a half hour in a cave entrance near some packrat nests.

Bears

Grizzlies have not roamed the mountains of New Mexico for decades, so bear attacks are extremely unlikely. Black bears are fairly common in many of the mountain ranges, although you are unlikely to encounter them. A little prevention will prevent any problems. Give bears a wide berth, especially those with cubs.

Put food and other smelly items, such as soap, toothpaste, and garbage, into a stuffsack and hang it from a tree well away from your tent. Hang it at least ten feet above the ground and out from the trunk. Let it dangle a few feet below the limb to prevent access from above. Hanging your food will also discourage rodents and raccoons. Leave your packs unzipped to prevent damage to them by a nosy animal. Never cook in your tent or keep food in your tent or sleeping bag. If a bear does take your food, don't even think about trying to get it back.

Snakes

The vast majority of snakes that you will encounter (usually you will see none) are nonpoisonous. On rare occasions you may encounter a rattlesnake, generally at elevations below about 7,000 feet. Most are not aggressive and will not strike unless stepped on or otherwise provoked. In daytime or cold weather they are usually holed up under rocks and in cracks. The most likely time to see them is in summer evenings in the desert. If you watch your step, don't hike at night, and don't put your hands or feet under rocks, ledges, and other places that you can't see, you should never have any problem. Don't hurt or kill any that you find. Remember, they are important predators.

If bitten, get medical help as soon as possible. Treatment methods are very controversial and beyond the scope of this book. Fortunately, the majority of bites do not inject a significant amount of venom. For basic treatment, tie a shoelace or other cord around the affected extremity between the bite and the rest of the body. Tie it only tight enough to dent the skin; don't cut off circulation. Apply ice if available. Get to a doctor. Do not use a snakebite kit unless you are very far from medical help.

Equipment

The most important outdoor equipment is probably your footwear. Hiking boots should be sturdy and comfortable. The lightweight boots are probably adequate for all but rugged trails and routes and for carrying heavy packs. Proper clothing, plenty of food and water, and a pack are other necessities. Other vital items for every trip include waterproof matches, raingear or some sort of emergency shelter, a pocketknife, a signal mirror and whistle, a first-aid kit, a detailed map, and a compass.

In general, all of your outdoor equipment should be as light and small as possible. Many excellent books and outdoor shops will help you select the proper boots, tents, sleeping bags, cooking utensils, and other equipment necessary for your hike.

Getting lost

Careful use of the maps and hike descriptions should prevent you from ever getting lost. However, if you should become lost or disoriented, immediately stop. Charging around blindly will only worsen the problem. Careful study of the map, compass, and surrounding landmarks will often reorient you. If you can retrace your route, follow it until you are oriented again. Don't proceed unless you are sure of your location. If you left travel plans with friends or family, rescuers should find you soon. In an emergency, follow a drainage downstream. In most areas, it will eventually lead you to a trail, road, or town. Remember, however, that it will probably take you farther away from rescuers. In a few of the largest wilderness areas, in particular the Gila Wilderness, it may take you deeper into the backcountry. Some of the drainages in the Gila go thirty or more miles before hitting civilization.

Use of signals may help rescuers find you. A series of three flashes or noises is the universal distress signal. Use the whistle or signal mirror. Provided that it can be done safely, a small smoky fire may help rescuers find you.

Hunting

National forest and BLM lands all generally allow hunting during the various seasons set up by state agencies. Fall in particular can bring out large numbers of deer and elk hunters. The seasons vary from year to year and in different parts of the state. Check with local ranger stations before your hike to determine what if any seasons might be in effect. If you hike during a hunting season, inquire locally to find areas that are less popular with hunters and wear bright colored clothing.

Most importantly, use of good judgment, adequate preparation, and common sense should keep all of your trips problem free.

HIKE 1 *UPPER AND LOWER FALLS*

General description: An easy day hike down Frijoles Canyon to two large waterfalls and the Rio Grande.
General location: Bandelier National Monument.
Length: About 4.5 miles round trip.
Elevation: 6,066-5,360 feet.
Maps: Bandelier National Monument "Trails Illustrated" topo map, Bandelier National Monument brochure, Frijoles 7.5-minute USGS quad.
Best season: All year.
Water availability: Frijoles Creek.
Special attractions: Two large waterfalls
Finding the trailhead: Bandelier National Monument lies just to the south of Los Alamos. Park at headquarters in the bottom of Frijoles Canyon.

The hike: Bandelier is famous for its extensive Indian ruins. Few visitors are aware that ninety percent of the park is virtually undisturbed wild land. Over seventy miles of maintained trails cross Bandelier. This hike is the park's most popular hike, other than the ruins trails, and makes an easy introduction to Bandelier's wilderness area.

Bandelier consists chiefly of a large sloping plateau, cut by deep, narrow canyons flowing to the Rio Grande. Massive volcanic eruptions from the huge crater in the Jemez Mountains built up a thick layer of consolidated volcanic ash, or tuff. To deposit such massive volumes of rock, the explosions had to have been magnitudes greater than those of Mt. St. Helens. The collapsed summit of the volcano, the present day Valle Grande, forms one of the largest calderas in the world. Elevations in the park range from 5,300 feet at the river to over 10,000 feet in the Jemez Mountains.

The permanent stream of Frijoles Creek has easily cut a deep canyon through the soft ash. At the Upper and Lower Falls, the stream encountered much harder layers of basalt. Since the creek was unable to erode the basalt as quickly as the surrounding tuff, waterfalls formed.

From the visitor center, cross the creek and walk downstream through the back country parking area to the well-marked trail. The trail descends at an easy grade along Frijoles Creek through lush riparian vegetation, such as willow, boxelder, and ponderosa pine. About 1.25 miles down the trail you reach Upper Falls. The trail overlooks the large waterfall from above, before making a short steep descent to the creek below the falls. The Lower Falls are only another 0.25 mile further, with a view from above. The Park Service does not allow hikers to approach the base of either waterfall because of the danger of rocks falling from the trail above.

After another short, steep descent at Lower Falls, the trail continues about 0.75 mile down the canyon to the Rio Grande. The last part of the hike is less shaded and hotter. At trail's end, the muddy Rio Grande flows by. Many of the trees are dead along the river, killed during the rare times that Cochiti Reservoir fills up. The lake, built in a fit of government excess, usually consists of more mud flats than water.

Upper Frijoles Falls is one of two large waterfalls along the Lower Falls hike at Bandelier National Monument.

HIKE 1 *UPPER AND LOWER FALLS*

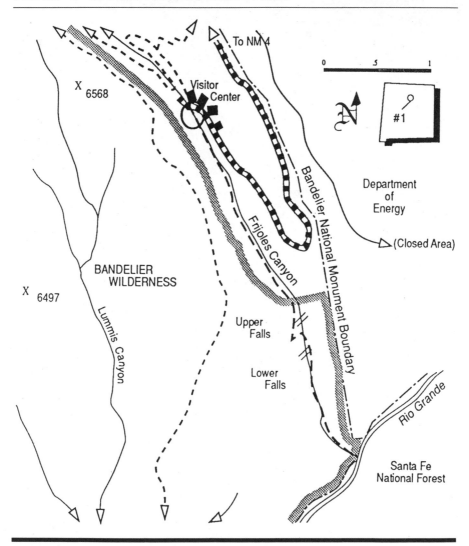

0   5   1

#1

To NM 4

Visitor Center

X 6568

X 6497

BANDELIER WILDERNESS

Lummis Canyon

Frijoles Canyon

Bandelier National Monument Boundary

Department of Energy

△ (Closed Area)

Upper Falls

Lower Falls

Rio Grande

Santa Fe National Forest

The hike can be quite hot in summer, especially on the uphill return leg. Be sure to carry plenty of water and start early, if possible. If necessary, water can be obtained from Frijoles Creek and purified, but, since the hike is short and the area very heavily used, carrying water is recommended.

The rebuilt kiva in Ceremonial Cave is one of many prehistoric ruins in Bandelier National Monument.

HIKE 2 *CEREMONIAL CAVE*

General description: An easy hike to an Indian ruin high above the floor of Frijoles Canyon.
General location: About fifteen miles south of Los Alamos.
Length: About two miles.
Elevation: 6,066-6,400 feet.
Maps: Bandelier National Monument "Trails Illustrated" topo map, Bandelier National Monument brochure, Frijoles 7.5-minute USGS quad.
Best season: Spring through fall.
Water availability: Visitor Center, Frijoles Creek.
Special attractions: Restored Indian kiva in a cave high above the canyon.
Finding the trailhead: The trail begins at the visitor center of Bandelier National Monument.

The hike: Frijoles Canyon, a narrow steep-walled canyon cut into the Pajarito Plateau, was home to a large community of Indians from about A.D. 1100

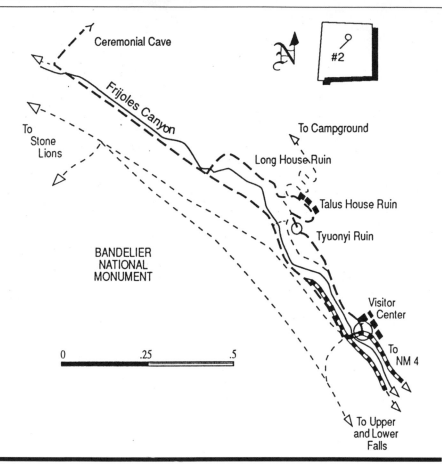

to 1550. The Indians raised corn, beans, and squash in the canyons and on the mesa tops of Bandelier and built impressive villages. The soft tuff (consolidated volcanic ash) was easy to carve, and the Indians honeycombed the cliffs of Frijole Canyon and other canyons for cave homes. Ancient Indian trails sometimes wore several feet deep into the tuff. The cause of abandonment of the villages is unknown. Archaeologists speculate that some combination of drought, soil depletion, marauding Indians, famine, or disease caused the Indians to leave.

To start, walk through the visitor center up the canyon on the main ruins trail. Stay on the north side of the creek. Within a few hundred yards, the trail forks. Keep right and walk through the large pueblo ruin of Tyuonyi. On the far side of Tyuonyi, the right fork will take you on the short loop through the Talus House Ruin. Stay left at the Frey Trail junction. It climbs up to the campground on the mesa. Immediately after, at the next junction, take the right fork up canyon to Long House. After passing Long House, you'll cross the permanent stream flowing down Frijoles Canyon to the Rio Grande. Continue on the trail up the canyon after crossing the creek.

The trail up the canyon is an easy walk along the stream through shady stands of ponderosa pine, box elder, and many other trees. About one-half mile up canyon from the first creek crossing, signs indicate the climb up to Ceremonial Cave, high above the creek bottom in the north wall of the canyon. A short series of Indian-style ladders and trail segments leads to the large natural shelter. The highlight of the cave is the restored kiva in the cave floor.

Return to the visitor center via the same route. At the junction to Long House and Tyuonyi, do not cross the creek. Rather, stay right and continue to follow the creek trail back to the visitor center, passing through the picnic area. The trail can be followed many miles farther upstream from Ceremonial Cave into the Bandelier Wilderness, an area of lush forests and beaver dams. Although water can be obtained from the creek, the canyon trail is heavily utilized up as far as Ceremonial Cave and carrying of water is recommended.

HIKE 3 *STONE LIONS*

General description: A strenuous two or three day hike to an ancient shrine deep in the Bandelier Wilderness.
General location: Bandelier National Monument.
Length: About eighteen miles round trip.
Elevation: 5,920-7,480 feet.
Maps: Bandelier National Monument ''Trails Illustrated'' topo map, Frijoles 7.5-minute USGS quad.
Best season: March through November.
Water availability: Upper Alamo Creek, Frijoles Creek.
Special attractions: Ancient Indian shrine and pueblo, deep gorges, solitude.
Permits: Required for overnight camping; obtain at monument visitor center.
Finding the trailhead: Bandelier National Monument lies south of Los Alamos. Park in the designated back country parking area at the visitor center.

The hike: The ruins in Frijoles Canyon are usually mobbed with people in summer, especially on weekends. Within minutes of starting this hike, however, you will leave the vast majority behind. This hike makes a large loop into the heart of the Bandelier Wilderness. Along the way it visits a large unexcavated pueblo, an ancient shrine unlike anything created elsewhere in the Southwest, running streams, and dense forest.

In summer, plan on using at least a gallon of water per day per person, especially on overnight hikes. The first half of the hike travels mostly through pinyon-juniper woodland and is very hot and exposed. The scrubby trees do not cast much shade on the trail itself. Try to get an early start to avoid the worst of the heat. The first water is not reached until Upper Alamo Canyon about nine miles into the hike, so prepare accordingly. The creek there is usually reliable, but inquire at the visitor center before starting. The hike is more difficult than the elevation and distance indicate because of several crossings of deep canyons. The first half of the loop is the hardest; it gets easier and more scenic the farther you go.

I foolishly didn't follow my own advice when I made the hike. I started alone at noon on a hot summer day with only three quarts of water and no means of purifying more. I did the entire eighteen miles in about seven hours, having run out of water far from the end. I arrived intact, but exhausted and dehydrated, just before dark. The one smart thing that I did do was to let friends know when I expected to be back, in case I didn't make it.

The trail is generally hikable all year, but in winter the hike can be very cold, especially at night. Snows, although not usually very deep, can obscure the trail on the flat mesa tops. If there is snow on the ground, it's best to go only if you are familiar with the trail and adept with a map and compass.

From the picnic area just across the creek from the visitor center, take the trail marked with signs for the Stone Lions. The first mile is a long, fairly steep climb up out of Frijoles Canyon. A side trail or two right after the start stay in the canyon bottom. Follow the Stone Lions signs. At a fork at the canyon rim, turn right toward the Lions and enter the wilderness. Another 100 yards further, the trail forks again. Go left toward the Lions. The trail traverses the relatively flat mesa top, crossing Lummis Canyon on the way.

Alamo Canyon is almost the halfway point on the way to the Lions. The narrow sheer-walled 600-foot deep canyon is spectacular but a major obstacle. The trail down is basically a set of rugged stairs, with the ascent only slightly better. Be sure to rest in the shade of the ponderosas lining the bottom. The canyon is usually dry.

After you struggle out of Alamo Canyon, there's only one more small canyon to cross before reaching Yapashi Ruins. The ruined walls and rubble of the ancient pueblo cover a large area on the left side of the trail. Don't disturb or remove any artifacts from the unexcavated site. Just down the trail at six miles is the Shrine of the Stone Lions. The two lions were carved hundreds of years ago by the early inhabitants of Bandelier. The soft tuff was easy to carve; unfortunately it also has eroded easily, making the lions barely recognizable. The two carvings are surrounded by a ring of stones. Local Pueblo Indians still consider the site sacred, so please don't disturb it. The Park Service doesn't permit camping within 0.25 mile of the Lions or the Yapashi Pueblo.

The trail forks at the Lions. Stay right, following the sign to Upper Crossing. A few hundred yards further, another trail forks off to the left, to Painted Cave. Stay right again, toward Upper Crossing. The next half mile climbs steeply up onto a higher mesa level, through an attractive shady canyon wooded largely with ponderosa pine. The canyon tops out in open ponderosa woodland that is much cooler than the first part of the hike. Here and there are open patches left by the large La Mesa Forest Fire of 1977. At the top of a divide at about 8 miles, good views open up of the high Jemez Mountains to the west. Also at the divide, another trail cuts left to Painted Cave. Bear right to Upper Crossing.

The crossing of Upper Alamo Canyon is much more pleasant than the lower crossing. The trail has a much gentler grade and is forested with ponderosa and Douglas fir. The stream at the bottom is usually reliable. If you camp here, move well away from the stream and practice good sanitation. Watch for poison ivy.

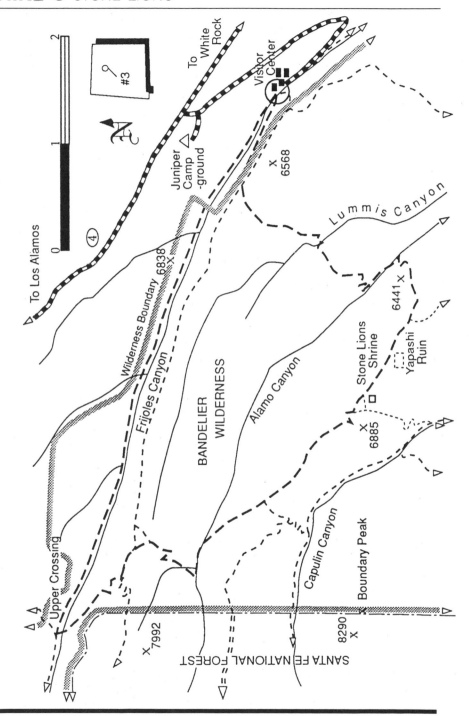

The climb out of Alamo Canyon is not too bad. Go left toward Upper Crossing at the next junction reached in a large old burned area. The right fork follows the rim of Frijole Canyon all the way back to the visitor center. It cuts off about three miles, if you're tired or short on time, but is much less scenic. Within another 0.25 mile, another fork cuts off to the right, following the same route as the previous fork. Bear left again toward Upper Crossing. After a short climb up through an old burned area, a third junction is reached. The left fork goes to the Alamo Springs trailhead. Turn right toward Upper Crossing. About 0.5 mile from the junction, the trail descends 600 feet into heavily wooded Frijoles Canyon.

From Upper Crossing, at twelve miles, only a long, gentle descent of six miles down Frijoles Canyon remains. At the junction in the canyon bottom, turn right toward park headquarters. Beware the poison ivy lining the trail for the first three miles or so. The canyon provides a lush, cool, peaceful walk beside a permanent stream. Don't camp at Upper Crossing; wait until you're at least 0.5 mile down the canyon. At Ceremonial Cave (See Hike 2), only a mile from the visitor center, the crowds will reappear, making the long peaceful hike worthwhile.

HIKE 4 *APACHE SPRING*

General description: An easy hike into the little-known, lush high country of the Bandelier Wilderness.
General location: Bandelier National Monument.
Length: About 5 miles round trip.
Elevation: 7,720-8,600 feet.
Maps: Bandelier National Monument "Trails Illustrated" topo map, Bland 7.5-minute USGS quad.
Best season: April through November.
Water availability: Apache Spring, Frijoles Creek.
Special attractions: Lush forests, permanent stream.
Permits: Required for camping; obtain at monument headquarters.
Finding the trailhead: From either Los Alamos or Bandelier National Monument headquarters, go to the junction of NM 4 and NM 501 along the north side of the monument. Go west 1.5 miles up into the mountains on NM 4 to the trailhead on the left (an unmarked parking area in front of a gate marked "Gate 10"). A forest service road goes off to the right across the highway from it.

The hike: Bandelier is well-known for its extensive Indian ruins, but few people leave the lower area of Frijoles Canyon surrounding the visitor center. Most people see only the scrubby pinyon-juniper woodland of the main ruins area, not realizing that most of the park lies in the Bandelier Wilderness. The park's back country rises as high as 10,199 feet and some is lushly wooded with aspen, fir, and spruce. This hike provides an introduction to the little-known high country of the monument.

The hike starts at about 8,180 feet. The first part of the hike follows an old dirt road, closed to vehicle traffic, through ponderosa pine and Douglas fir. Very quickly the road drops down to a meadow with a couple of picnic tables.

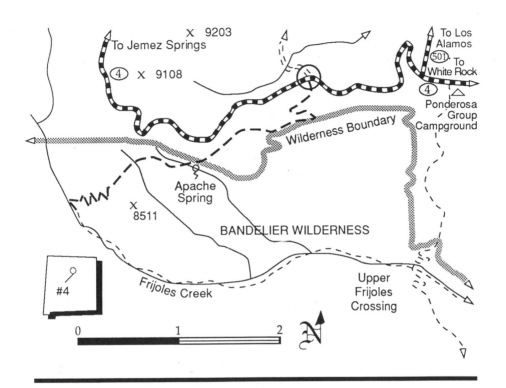

It then climbs gradually up to a ridgetop and hits a four-way junction. Turn right onto the most-used route, marked by a sign to Apache Spring. A few recovering burned patches mark the upper extent of the large 1977 La Mesa Fire. At about 1.25 miles, the old road ends at the Bandelier Wilderness boundary. Signs indicate the boundary and trail distances.

The trail drops down a short distance into a small canyon. At the canyon bottom, a sign marks the very short side trail downstream to Apache Spring. If you obtain water, purify it. Take the trail up the canyon bottom, following the sign to Upper Crossing. About 0.25 mile up, a faint trail crosses the main trail. Ignore it and continue up the canyon bottom. The trail reaches its high point shortly after climbing up out of the canyon. The trail follows a relatively level path through woods until it abruptly reaches the rim of Frijole Canyon at about two miles. The next half mile is the only difficult part of the hike, as the trail steeply descends 750 feet to the bottom of the canyon.

The canyon bottom is lushly wooded and has a permanent bubbling stream. Return the same way you came, unless you want a longer hike. The easy trail in the canyon bottom can be followed downstream as far as desired. Some inactive beaver dams will be encountered as you go. Beware the thriving poison ivy lining much of the trail in the creek bottom. A loop can be made by following the canyon trail down the three-plus miles to Upper Crossing, climbing out of the canyon 1.5 miles to Ponderosa Campground on NM 4, and walking 1.7 miles back up NM 4 past the NM 501 junction to your car. With a car shuttle, you can hike the long, but easy, six miles from Upper Crossing all the way down Frijoles Creek to the monument visitor center (See Hike 3).

HIKE 5 *TSANKAWI RUIN*

General description: An easy hike along ancient Indian trails to a large unexcavated ruin in Bandelier National Monument.
General location: Bandelier National Monument.
Length: About 1.5 miles round trip.
Elevation: 6,490-6,680 feet.
Maps: Bandelier National Monument "Trails Illustrated" topo map, Tsankawi trail guide, White Rock 7.5-minute USGS quad.
Best season: All year.
Water availability: None.
Special attractions: Indian ruins, ancient trails, petroglyphs, views.
Finding the trailhead: Drive about one mile southwest on NM 4 from its intersection with NM 502 about six miles east of Los Alamos. Stop at the marked parking area on the left side of the road. Tsankawi ruin is a detached unit of the main park twelve miles away.

The hike: The separate Bandelier unit of Tsankawi contains a large mesa with surrounding valley land. Pinyon pine and juniper, along with a scattering of ponderosa, wood the area. This hike is one of the shortest in the book, but has many unique features.

Much of the trail follows the prehistoric routes up onto the mesa top. Thousands of people's feet, using the trails for centuries, have worn deeply into the soft volcanic tuff. In places the old trails cut several several feet into the rock. The large pueblo on the mesa top was probably built during the 1400s and occupied until the late 1500s.

The trail climbs up to the mesa top in two steps. After the first level, the trail forks, forming a loop. Stay left and climb up onto the mesa. A ladder must be climbed up the final ledge to the top. The mesa top itself has a very flat surface. The 350-room pueblo lies in the middle of the long narrow mesa. Only tumbled-down walls and a tremendous view of the Rio Grande Valley remain. Please don't disturb any of the ruins or artifacts.

After passing the pueblo, the trail drops down another ladder onto a ledge on the side of the mesa. Caves carved into the soft tuff line the cliffs by the ladder. The pueblo people built masonry buildings in front of the caves and lived in them. The trail curves back around the mesa, following ancient trails to the end of the loop. At sunset, watch the towering Sangre de Cristo Mountains across the Rio Grande Valley turn red and orange just before the sun drops below the horizon. Be sure to leave right afterwards, since the ruins close at dusk.

The feet of numerous prehistoric residents wore deep trails into the soft volcanic tuff of Tsankawi Mesa.

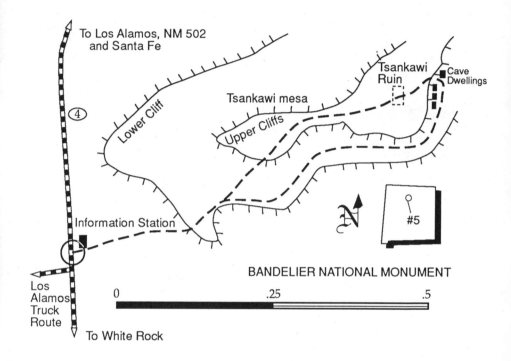

HIKE 6 MCCAULEY HOT SPRINGS

General description: An easy day hike to a large hot spring in the Jemez Mountains.
General location: About thirty-five miles west of Los Alamos.
Length: About 3.5 miles round trip.
Elevation: 6,760-7,340 feet.
Maps: Santa Fe National Forest, Jemez Springs and Redondo Peak 7.5 USGS quad.
Best season: All year.
Water availability: McCauley Hot Spring.
Special attractions: Hot spring.
Finding the trailhead: From the junction of NM 501 and NM 4 about five miles southwest of Los Alamos, drive west 27.8 miles on NM 4 up into the mountains. Park at the Battleship Rock Picnic Ground.

The hike: A huge caldera, created when an enormous volcano collapsed, forms the heart of the Jemez Mountains. Ash erupting from the mountain covered 400 square miles to depths of 1000 feet. The crater rim is about fifteen miles in diameter, one of the largest in the world. Although the volcano is no longer active, magma still lies fairly close to the surface under the mountains. The hot rock heats groundwater, which surfaces as numerous hot springs throughout the mountains. In the search for potential geothermal energy sources, a number of test wells have been drilled in the Jemez.

This popular hike goes to a large hot spring, ideal for relaxing regardless of the time of year. Snows in winter may temporarily make the trail hard to find, but nothing feels better than a hot soak on a cold day.

Walk to the back of the picnic ground under the "prow" of the huge formation known as Battleship Rock. Trail 137 starts up the East Fork of the Jemez River from behind a round, gazebo-like picnic shelter. A "Trail 137" sign marks the spot. The trail follows along the left bank of the river for the first 0.25 mile or so. Watch for Trail 137 signs to help you find your way through the maze of social trails along the heavily used creek. An old trail climbs up to the spring just after you pass the base of Battleship Rock, but the new trail is easier. The new trail continues a little farther up the canyon bottom before beginning the climb up away from the river. A few large switchbacks help moderate the fairly steep grade. After you get part-way up the side of the south facing slope of the canyon, the confusing side trails disappear.

At about the halfway point, the trail's grade lessens, making the rest of the walk very easy. Shortly before the spring, observant hikers will notice the ruined walls and rubble of an old Indian pueblo near the trail. Please don't disturb the site.

The spring, at about 1.75 miles, lies on a ponderosa-covered slope. The clear sandy-bottomed pool, created by a large rock wall, is about thirty feet across and three feet deep. Relax and enjoy the flowing warm water with the guppies, tetras, and other tropical fish that people have introduced.

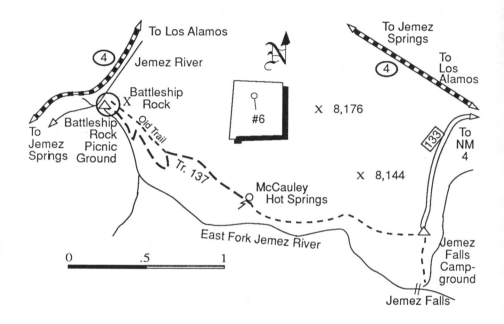

Be sure not to get the pool water up inside your nose. On very rare occasions at other hot springs in the west, an amoeba has been known to pass through the mucous membranes, causing a very serious illness. If you're not too relaxed by the warm water, consider following Trail 137 another 1.75 miles to spectacular Jemez Falls.

HIKE 7 *JEMEZ RIVER*

General description: An easy day hike along the East Fork of the Jemez River.
General location: About twenty-five miles west of Los Alamos.
Length: About three miles round trip.
Elevation: 8,230-7,920 feet.
Maps: Santa Fe National Forest, Redondo Peak 7.5 minute USGS quad.
Best season: April through November.
Water availability: Jemez River.
Special attractions: Mountain stream in a narrow canyon, cross country ski route.
Finding the trailhead: From the junction of NM 4 and NM 501, about five miles southwest of Los Alamos, drive west 18.1 miles on NM 4 up into the mountains. Stop at the well-marked East Fork trailhead parking area.

The hike: The East Fork of the Jemez River drains a large part of Valle Grande. The large circular valley, ringed with peaks as high as 11,500 feet, formed after an enormous eruption several million years ago. The explosion blew the heart of the mountain out, causing it to collapse into a large caldera, or crater. Eventually, several streams and rivers, such as the East Fork, cut through the crater wall. This hike follows an easy loop along part of the river. The trail is new and doesn't show on maps. Prepare to wade for a short part of the hike.

From the trailhead, follow the Trail 137 signs through second-growth ponderosa across a fairly level hilltop. Blue plastic diamonds nailed to trees mark the route along an abandoned logging road. The diamonds mark the route for cross country ski use in winter.

About 0.25 mile along the trail, a less-used blue diamond route forks to the right. Stay left on the main route. At just over one mile, Trail 137 forks. Go left, downhill, following the sign to East Fork Box. The trail descends steeply through dense Douglas fir about another 0.25 mile to a second junction. The left fork, Trail 137A, is the proper route, going to the marked "East Fork River." The sign at the junction says two miles back to the East Fork Trailhead, but it's really less than 1.5 miles. If you have time, be sure to make the short side hike to the right to the East Fork Box. At the Box, the river squeezes into a narrow rocky gorge, impassable because of deep pools and waterfalls.

The left fork reaches the river after another short steep descent. A small footbridge crosses the small river, at least until the next flood washes it away. Follow the river downstream along its narrow, but lush grassy bottom. Soon the river narrows into a short section of small gorge. Plan to get your feet wet; the trail crosses from bank to bank in the rocky defile. In cold weather bring an extra pair of shoes. The canyon then widens for the last stretch before crossing NM 4 at about 2.25 miles. On summer weekends, you'll encounter quite a few people on the last part of the trail. At the highway, hike left up the road about a half mile to the trailhead or retrace the same route for your return.

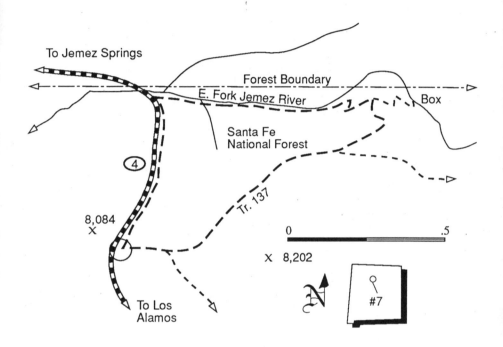

To Jemez Springs

Forest Boundary

E. Fork Jemez River

Box

Santa Fe
National Forest

4

8,084
X

Tr. 137

X 8,202

0   .5

To Los
Alamos

N

#7

HIKE 8 *SAN PEDRO PARKS*

General description: An easy two or three day hike into the lush meadows and forests of the San Pedro Parks Wilderness.

General location: About ninety-five miles northwest of Albuquerque.

Length: About fifteen miles round trip.

Elevation: 9,200-10,300 feet.

Maps: San Pedro Parks Wilderness, Santa Fe National Forest, Nacimiento Peak 7.5-minute USGS quad.

Best season: May through October.

Water availability: Rio de las Vacas, Clear Creek.

Special attractions: Large meadows, solitude, winter cross-country ski potential.

Finding the trailhead: From Cuba, drive east on NM 126 up into the mountains about six miles to the end of the pavement. About 0.25 mile from the end of the pavement, turn left onto gravel FR 70 and drive 2.8 miles to the parking lot, marked with signs for Trail 51 and the San Pedro Parks Wilderness. The 1975 Santa Fe National Forest map does not show FR 70 properly; reportedly a revised map is in the works.

From Los Alamos, start at the junction of NM 4 and NM 501 a few miles southwest of town. Drive west on NM 4 into the mountains for 24.5 miles to the junction of NM 126. Turn right onto NM 126 and follow it 29.8 very scenic miles to the turnoff of FR 70 above. The first nine miles of NM 126 is paved, the remainder dirt. The gravel surface is generally good in dry conditions, but a mile or two in the middle are treacherous in wet weather. The dirt section of NM 126 is closed in winter.

The hike: This is one of my favorite hikes in New Mexico, in part because it is so different from most of the state's mountain areas. The 41,132-acre San Pedro Parks Wilderness is basically a big, relatively level area of forest and meadows. Crystal-clear, slow moving mountain streams meander down through broad marshy valley bottoms. Multiple large meadows give the area a manicured, park-like atmosphere. Instead of having a few high peaks, much of the entire wilderness lies at about 10,000 feet. No sheer cliffs or jagged peaks break up the terrain. Most New Mexico mountains are very steep, with level areas few and far between.

Because the area is not very steep and mountainous, hiking is very easy, even over long distances. Additionally, plentiful water is available in the many creeks. This fifteen-mile hike gains only about 1,100 feet and can be done in a day fairly easily by someone in reasonable shape. However, you'll regret not spending two or three days once you see it. Potential campsites are almost innumerable.

From the parking lot, follow Trail 51, the Vacas Trail, through spruce and fir about 0.75 mile to Cienega Gregorio Lake. On summer weekends, the lake and trail to it can be busy. Once you leave the lake behind, you probably will not see many hikers. Weekdays are even better. When I did the hike on a summer weekday, I only saw one couple and one family in the entire thirteen miles of hiking past the lake.

Boulders dot one of many meadows in the San Pedro Parks Wilderness.

Follow the trail around the right (east) side of the small lake and away to the north. A little past the lake, a trail forks back to the lake on the left. Keep going north. At almost two miles you'll hit Clear Creek, marked by a sign. The trail follows the creek for over a mile, before climbing out a tributary into a long, flat wooded stretch. Here and there a few faint old trails fork off, but the main trail is obvious.

Occasionally the trail crosses marshy meadows and creek bottoms. It's sometimes difficult to keep your feet dry during the crossings, especially right after the snow melts in the spring and after late summer rains. For overnight trips, you might want to carry an extra pair of tennis shoes. The trail sometimes gets faint in the marshy areas. Look carefully for the trail on the opposite side of the meadow and you shouldn't have any problem. Also, wooden posts often mark the way in confusing sections. The junctions are generally fairly well marked, but having a copy of the San Pedro Parks Wilderness map will help immensely in avoiding any confusion in the large open meadow areas.

At about 5.25 miles, the trail reaches the Rio de las Vacas. After this point, you will mostly be hiking across meadows. Be careful of lightning in the open areas, especially in late summer. Right after crossing the stream, Palomas Trail 50, forks off to the right. Turn left up the creek, staying on Trail 51 toward San Pedro Park. About 0.25 mile up the creek, the Anastacio Trail 435, forks

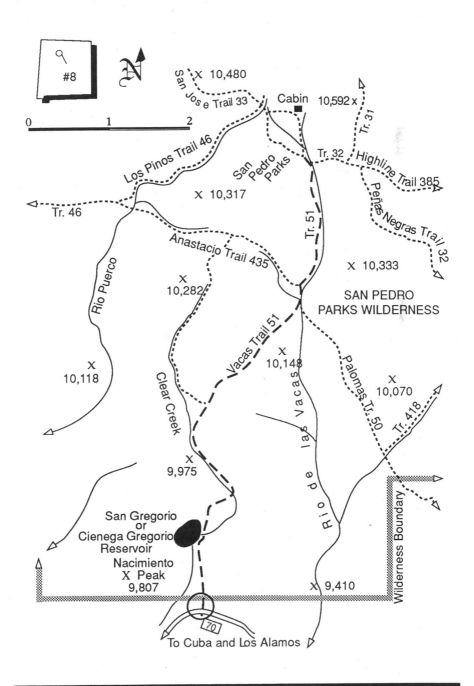

off to the left. Stay right on Trail 51 toward San Pedro Park. The rest of the hike follows the broad, grassy creek bottom of the Rio de las Vacas.

At about 7.5 miles, the trail reaches the junction with the Penas Negras Trail, 32, on the right. From here, either return the same way, or continue as far as time and energy allow. By adding an easy three or four miles, a loop can be done by following Trail 51 a mile further up to Trail 46. Turn left on Trail 46, follow it for about 2.5 miles, and turn left again on the Anastacio Trail, 435, to make a loop back to the 5.5-mile point on Trail 51.

HIKE 9 *SANTA FE BALDY*

General description: A moderately strenuous day hike or moderate overnight hike to a high summit of the Pecos Wilderness.
General location: About fifteen miles northeast of Santa Fe.
Length: About fourteen miles round trip.
Elevation: 10,300-12,622 feet.
Maps: Pecos Wilderness, Santa Fe National Forest, Aspen Basin 7.5-minute USGS quad.
Best season: Late May through November.
Water availability: Rio Nambe.
Special attractions: Tremendous 360-degree views of the Sangre de Cristo Mountains, Jemez Mountains, and Rio Grande Valley.
Finding the trailhead: Take State Highway 475 (Hyde Park Road) from Santa Fe about fifteen miles to the parking area just below the ski area. Signs indicate the trailhead.

The hike: Santa Fe Baldy is one of a line of high peaks along the divide between the Rio Grande and Pecos River drainages. At 12,622 feet, the peak rises well above timberline. Its rounded, "bald" appearance probably led to its name. The prominent summit gives one of the best views possible of the 223,000-acre Pecos Wilderness. The Wilderness and the surrounding Santa Fe National Forest, divided between the Sangre de Cristo and Jemez Mountains, have 1,000 miles of mapped trails.

The Windsor Trail (254) is well-marked at the parking area just below the Santa Fe Ski Basin. The wide, popular trail climbs steeply for the first half-mile to the Pecos Wilderness Boundary. From the boundary, on a ridge top, the trail descends slightly through lush Douglas fir, spruce, and aspen to the Rio Nambe at about 2.5 miles. A short distance past the wilderness boundary, you will pass the lightly-used Trail 403 forking to the left. The Rio Nambe is the best source of water along the route.

From the Rio Nambe, the trail climbs gradually again, crossing the east fork of the river at about four miles. This is the last reliable water source. The forest begins to thin in this stretch of trail, offering good views of Baldy above to the north and the Rio Grande Valley to the west. About one-half mile beyond the river fork, the Rio Nambe Trail (160) joins from the left. The area around the east fork of the river and the Trail 160 junction makes an ideal camping area on overnight trips.

HIKE 9 *SANTA FE BALDY*

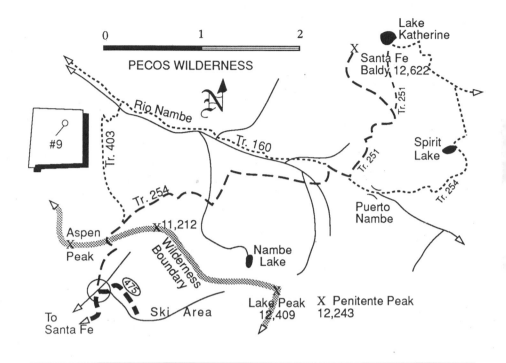

Just beyond the Rio Nambe Trail junction, Trail 254 turns sharply from northwest to southeast. About 0.25 mile from the Trail 160 junction, turn left onto Trail 251 to Lake Katherine. Trail 251 climbs steadily up to the crest of the ridge, reaching an elevation of about 11,600 feet. Leave the trail at the top and climb the crest of the ridge to the left (north). Stay on the crest of the ridge until you reach the summit in about a mile. This is the steepest part of the hike, with a gain of about 1,000 feet.

From the summit, virtually the entire wilderness area can be seen to the north and east. The Sandia Mountains are visible far to the south and the Jemez Mountains lie across the Rio Grande Valley to the west. On clear days, peaks in Colorado are visible.

Much of the climb from the pass is above timberline and exposed. Be sure to carry rain gear and warm clothes even in summer. Whether you camp below the peak or do the trip as a day hike, try to get an early enough start to reach the summit by noon. Thunderstorms can develop with astonishing speed, especially in late summer afternoons. Getting caught in a lightning storm above timberline is an experience you'll never forget.

The return follows the same route. A more extended backpack can be made by continuing down the east side of the pass to Lake Katherine, Spirit Lake, or many of the other lakes and streams of the Pecos River drainage. The hiking season varies depending on the amount of snow received during the winter.

HIKE 10 *TESUQUE CREEK*

General description: An easy dayhike to a rushing mountain stream within minutes of Santa Fe.
General location: About ten miles northeast of Santa Fe.
Length: About four miles round trip.
Elevation: 8,920-8,280 feet.
Maps: Pecos Wilderness, Santa Fe National Forest, Aspen Basin and McClure Reservoir 7.5-minute USGS quads.
Best season: May through November.
Water availability: Tesuque Creek.
Special attractions: Mountain stream, dense forest.
Finding the trailhead: From Santa Fe, take NM 475 up toward the ski area. On the left, just past Hyde State Park, lies the paved parking area for the trailhead. Signs mark it as the trailhead for Borrego Trail 150.

The hike: This hike's proximity to Santa Fe is part of its attraction. Within twenty minutes of leaving the Plaza, you'll be strolling through Douglas fir, spruce, and aspen. The hike touches only a tiny fraction of the Santa Fe National Forest and its 1,000 miles of trails. Many of the other hikes in this book are in the Santa Fe National Forest.

From the parking lot, the well-used trail drops down into a wooded, dry creek bottom. It follows the creek down for about 0.5 mile to a junction. Go right at the junction, staying on Trail 150. The trail climbs up a small tributary to a low saddle, before dropping down again. After a fairly steep descent into another tributary, the trail reaches Tesuque Creek, announced in advance by the roar of rushing water. Be sure to purify any water taken from the stream.

At the creek, Trail 150 merges into Trail 254, the Winsor Trail, about 1.5 miles from the trailhead. To the right, the Winsor Trail climbs up to the ski area and miles beyond into the Pecos Wilderness. Go left, following Trail 254 down Tesuque Creek for about a mile to the junction with Trail 182 on the left.

Follow Trail 182 up a dry tributary for about a mile to its junction with Trail 150. The loop is now completed. Turn right and retrace your route up 150 to the parking lot. The hike makes an ideal quick escape from Santa Fe. My wife and I did the hike late one summer afternoon after a long tiring drive up to Santa Fe from Texas.

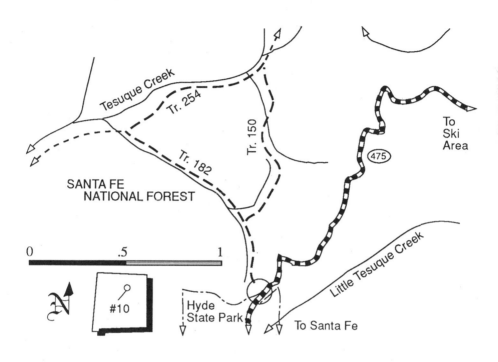

HIKE 11 *LAKE KATHERINE*

General description: A strenuous day hike or overnight trip to a high alpine lake at the base of Santa Fe Baldy.
General location: About forty miles northeast of Santa Fe.
Length: About eleven miles round trip.
Elevation: 8,440-11,742 feet.
Maps: Pecos Wilderness, Santa Fe National Forest, Cowles and Aspen Basin 7.5-minute USGS quads.
Best season: June through October.
Water availability: Winsor Creek, Lake Katherine.
Special attractions: Large alpine lake in a glacial cirque.
Finding the trailhead: From Pecos, drive about twenty miles north on NM 63 to the summer home area at Cowles. The pavement ends and a gravel surface begins after about fourteen miles. In Cowles turn left, crossing the Pecos River, to the marked Winsor Creek Trailhead on FR 121. Drive 1.3 miles to the trailhead at the end of the road. Contrary to what most maps still show, Winsor Creek is no longer a campground; it's only a trailhead.

The hike: Lake Katherine is a popular destination for hikers in the Santa Fe area. The large, crystal-clear lake nestles in the bottom of a valley at the eastern base of Santa Fe Baldy. The glacial valley, or cirque, was carved out of the bedrock by glaciers in recent ice ages. The rock removed by the flowing ice was deposited in a long narrow mound, or moraine, at the bottom end of the glacier. The massive pile of rubble created a natural dam at the mouth of the cirque and the lake was born.

The lake lies at timberline, with the cliffs and slopes rising above mostly either bare or covered with fragile tundra. The lake lies at a high elevation and requires a climb of over 3,000 feet to reach. Be sure that you are in good condition before attempting the hike. Take warm clothes and rain gear any time of year. Thunderstorms rise quickly, especially in late summer.

From the trailhead at the end of the road, Trail 254 follows lush Winsor Creek upstream on the right bank. A little less than a mile up, the trail crosses the creek to the south bank. The trail forks just across the creek (unmarked). The right fork, Trail 261, continues up the creek, climbing high on the left bank. It is the shortest, steepest route to Katherine and Stewart lakes. A ranger told me that the Forest Service planned to abandon the trail. As of the summer of 1990, the trail was in good condition. Eventually deadfalls will probably make the route too much trouble. The left fork, the continuation of Trail 254, climbs up toward the lake at a much easier grade, but probably adds three miles to the climb. Eventually it may be necessary to take Trail 254, but this hike will use Trail 261. Both trails are still marked on the Pecos Wilderness map.

After a long steady climb out of Winsor Creek, Trail 261 rejoins Trail 254 at about three miles. For variety, Trail 254 could be used on your descent. After the junction the grade moderates. Go right on Trail 254 about 0.5 mile to the junction with Trail 251. Trail 254 rejoins Winsor Creek at the junction. Go left, upstream, on combined Trail 254 and 251, following the sign to Lake Katherine. Trail 251 to the right goes to Stewart Lake (See Hike 12).

Formed by glaciers, spectacular Lake Katherine lies at the foot of Santa Fe Baldy.

From the Stewart Lake junction, the trail begins to climb a little more steeply again. At about four miles, Trail 254 splits off to the left to Spirit Lake. Go right on Trail 251 to Lake Katherine, as directed by the sign. The trail now begins to climb and switchback in earnest as the air gets thinner. Spirit Lake is a considerably easier and faster hike from here than Lake Katherine. Some potential campsites can be found in the area of the junction.

As you climb toward Lake Katherine, the dense forest begins to thin and the trees become smaller. After a long arduous climb, with views opening up to the south and east, the trail reaches a very small lake tucked into a deep valley. One last grunt up the steep slope above the small lake brings you to Lake Katherine at about 5.5 miles.

Sheer cliffs rise above the large, clear lake. Boulders and rubble spill down the slopes from the base of the cliffs. Snow and ice persists through the summer in drifts and sheltered crevices. A few hardy spruce trees lie scattered around the shores. Pikas chirp warnings from their hideouts in the rocky talus slopes, while marmots looking for an easy lunch approach hikers.

Santa Fe Baldy towers above the lake, poking high into the deep blue sky. The keen-eyed may observe a few hikers on the summit (See Hike 9). The peak can be approached from the lake by continuing up Trail 251 to the crest and, from there, following the crest up to the top.

If you camp at Lake Katherine, be sure to set up on slopes below the lake, outside of the drainage basin. Use care in sanitation. The vegetation at that altitude is very fragile, so try to camp and walk only on bare areas. Be sure to bring warm clothes and sleeping bags.

HIKE 12 *STEWART LAKE*

General description: A moderate day hike or overnight trip to a beautiful lake in the Pecos Wilderness.
General location: About forty miles northeast of Santa Fe.
Length: About ten miles round trip.
Elevation: 8,180-10,232 feet.
Maps: Pecos Wilderness, Santa Fe National Forest, Cowles 7.5-minute USGS quad.
Best season: June through October.
Water availability: Stewart Lake.
Special attractions: A natural mountain lake.
Finding the trailhead: Follow the same directions to Cowles as Hike 11. After turning left onto FR 121, stop right away at the Cowles Campground on the left, rather than following the road to its end at the Winsor Creek trailhead.

The hike: Stewart Lake is a beautiful small lake created by glaciers during the recent ice ages. A small earthen dam enlarges the natural lake somewhat. Unlike the much higher Lake Katherine (See Hike 11), Stewart Lake is surrounded by heavy forest. Although the lake requires moderate effort to reach, it is one of the easiest alpine lakes to hike to in the Pecos Wilderness. Thus it is a popular hike, especially on summer weekends.

The trail starts across the road from Cowles Campground. It climbs up the hill a short distance to Trail 271. To the right, Trail 271 goes to Panchuela Campground. Go left and start the long steady climb to the west. The trail slowly climbs higher with few switchbacks. The grade is steady, but relatively easy for almost the entire hike. As the trail climbs high above Winsor Creek, better and better views open up to the south and east. The trail passes through a lush forest of Douglas fir and aspen.

Finally, at about 4.5 miles, your trail intersects Trail 251 after a very short descent. Go left on Trail 251 to Stewart Lake. The last half mile to Stewart Lake is relatively level. Along the way, you'll pass a pond on the right, set in a enormous, flat, marshy meadow.

If possible try to camp for a couple of nights at Stewart Lake. Relax, fish, or day hike up to Lake Katherine, Spirit Lake, or Lake Johnson (See Hike 11). Stewart Lake is fairly heavily used, so be sure to camp well away from the lake on bare ground out of the lake's drainage basin. Be careful with sanitation.

The same route can be followed back down or you can continue along Trail 251 about 0.5 mile to the junction with Trail 254. Follow Trail 254 and 261 down to Winsor Creek as described in the Lake Katherine hike. Then walk down FR 121 about 1.25 miles to the trailhead. Both routes are fairly similar in length.

HIKE 13 CAVE CREEK

General description: An easy Pecos Wilderness hike through lush forest to a series of caves.
General location: Forty miles northeast of Santa Fe.
Length: Five miles round trip.
Elevation: 8,320-9,020 feet.
Maps: Pecos Wilderness, Santa Fe National Forest, Cowles 7.5-minute USGS quad.
Best season: June through October.
Water availability: Hike follows permanent stream.
Special attractions: Lush forest and trout stream; caves with flowing stream.
Finding the trailhead: From Pecos (about twenty miles east of Santa Fe), drive up the Pecos River valley on State Highway 63 to the summer home area of Cowles. Be careful in Pecos itself; the town is a speed trap. The last few miles of road are dirt, but are easily passable by any vehicle except in winter. Turn left at the small fishing lake in Cowles and cross the Pecos River, following the signs to Winsor Creek and Panchuela Campgrounds. Right after crossing the river, turn right on the Panchuela Campground Road. After driving through a guest ranch, you'll reach the campground and wilderness parking area at the end of the road.

The hike: The Sangre de Cristo Mountains are the largest and highest mountains in New Mexico. Rising from foothills east of Santa Fe and west of Las Vegas, the mountains continue north for over 200 miles, well into Colorado. According to legend, the mountains were named for the "blood of Christ" by a dying Spanish priest during the Pueblo Revolt of 1680 when the mountains turned red at sunset.

The Santa Fe National Forest, the second oldest national forest in the United States, was created by President Harrison in 1892 as the Pecos River Forest Reserve. Part of the forest was protected as the 223,000-acre Pecos Wilderness in 1933. The wilderness contains over 150 miles of streams, many alpine lakes, and several glacier-sculpted peaks over 13,000 feet high.

Start the hike by walking from the wilderness parking area into the Panchuela Creek Campground. The trail (288) leads out of the center of the campground by crossing the creek to the north, or right, bank. The trail follows rushing Panchuela Creek upstream for about 1.5 miles. At times the trail lies next to the creek; at others it climbs fifty or 100 feet above. A short distance upstream from the campground, Trail 259 forks off to the right and climbs out of Panchuela Creek. Stay left on trail following the creek. Another trail merges from the left from the direction of the campground. It's simply an alternate route back to the trailhead and campground.

The trail passes through lush forests of Douglas fir, aspen, and blue spruce. Willows and other deciduous shrubs and trees line the banks of the clear, rushing stream. Trout flit out of sight under rocks and banks at your approach.

After about 1.5 miles, the trail turns west into a tributary, Cave Creek, while Panchuela Creek continues north. As you continue up Cave Creek, you will suddenly notice the silence. The roar of rushing water, present for the entire hike, is missing. Except during times of heavy runoff, the stream is dry.

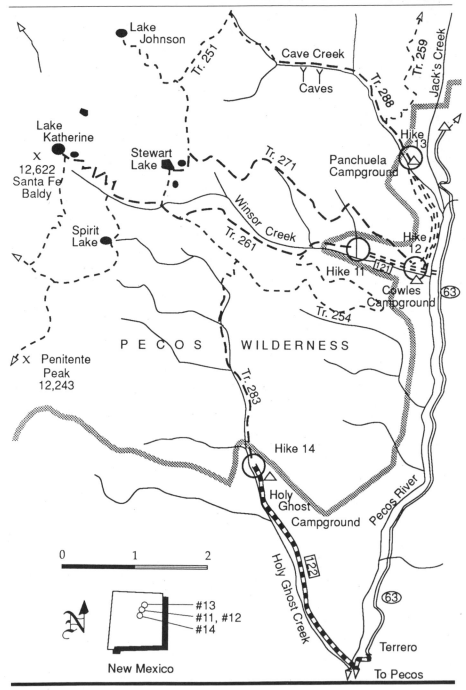

Lake Johnson

Tr. 251

Cave Creek

Tr. 259

Jack's Creek

Caves

Tr. 288

Lake Katherine

Stewart Lake

Tr. 271

Hike 13

X 12,622 Santa Fe Baldy

Panchuela Campground

Winsor Creek

Spirit Lake

Tr. 261

Hike 12

121

Hike 11

Cowles Campground

63

Tr. 254

X Penitente Peak 12,243

P E C O S   W I L D E R N E S S

Tr. 283

Hike 14

Holy Ghost Campground

Pecos River

0   1   2

Holy Ghost Creek

122

N

#13
#11, #12
#14

Terrero

63

New Mexico

To Pecos

The permanent Pecos Wilderness stream of Cave Creek flows through a cave for part of its length.

Continue up the trail, watching the creek on your left closely. Soon the sound of running water reappears and a cave mouth appears on the left bank of the creek. The stream disappears into the cave and flows underground for some distance, drying up the normal creek bed. Continue upstream along the trail a short distance farther to two even larger cave entrances taking the bulk of the creek flow. The caves can easily be entered here. Be sure not to enter alone and to wear hard hats and have three sources of light for each person. Use care; the caves are cold and wet with slippery rock and steep drops. Whether you enter the caves or not, the hike is a beautiful introduction to the Pecos Wilderness.

From the caves, follow the trail a short distance further upstream to the confluence of Cave Creek and Rito Oscuro. Ferns flourish among the aspens in a small parklike area at the fork in the creek. Return to the trailhead via the same route. Time and energy allowing, the trail can be followed much farther to such destinations as Horsethief Meadow and alpine Lake Johnson and Stewart Lake.

HIKE 14 *HOLY GHOST CREEK*

General description: An easy day hike up a rushing trout stream through the lush forest of the Pecos Wilderness.
General location: About forty miles northeast of Santa Fe.
Length: About five miles round trip.
Elevation: 8,240-9,180 feet.
Maps: Pecos Wilderness, Santa Fe National Forest, Cowles 7.5-minute USGS quad.
Best season: May through November.
Water availability: Holy Ghost Creek.
Special attractions: Tumbling mountain stream, beautiful forest.
Finding the trailhead: From Pecos, go about fourteen miles north up the Pecos River valley on NM 63 to the marked Holy Ghost Campground turnoff. Turn left onto the narrow paved road (FR 122) and follow it about three miles to the end at the campground.

The hike: Holy Ghost Creek provides a pleasant, easy introduction to the Pecos Wilderness. Although this hike is not especially long or difficult, it gives a good feel for the many permanent streams that flow out of the Sangre de Cristo Mountains.

Trail 283 starts from the end of the road at the upper end of the campground. The last stretch of road goes to the group campground and is usually closed, so park below it. The trail follows the stream through lush forests of aspen, Douglas fir, and ponderosa, crossing the creek occasionally. At about 1.5 miles, a large tributary joins the creek on the left and the trail makes a short, steep climb up onto the left bank. At about two miles it again rejoins the creek at another left-hand tributary.

The trail again makes a short, steep climb up the left bank and then rejoins the creek another 0.5 mile further at the end of the hike. Beyond this point the trail then crosses to the right bank and begins to climb completely out of the creek drainage, eventually joining Trail 254 on the ridge top. For the energetic, Trail 254 can be followed all the way to Lake Katherine, Santa Fe Baldy, Stewart Lake, and many other destinations. See Hikes 9, 11, and 12.

HIKE 15 *HERMIT PEAK*

General description: A strenuous day hike to the rocky summit of a prominent Pecos Wilderness peak.

General location: About twenty miles northwest of Las Vegas.

Length: About eight miles round trip.

Elevation: 7,500-10,212 feet.

Maps: Pecos Wilderness, Santa Fe National Forest, El Porvenir 7.5-minute USGS quad.

Best season: May through November.

Water availability: Trailhead, Hermit Spring.

Special attractions: Views.

Finding the trailhead: From the center of Las Vegas, take NM 65 west. The route is poorly marked; ask for directions if you have trouble finding it. After you pass the Armand Hammer World College, the road, while still paved, becomes narrow, windy, and mountainous. Be careful on the many blind curves. The road passes through the villages of Gallinas and El Porvenir. At about 14.5 miles, the road splits. Go right to El Porvenir Campground, as marked. Park in the parking lot at the entrance of the campground at about seventeen miles.

The hike: Hermit Peak anchors the far southeastern arm of the Pecos Wilderness. Although the summit has a broad, flat top, towering cliffs dominate its eastern escarpment. The sheer walls give the peak a notable appearance, making it recognizable miles away out on the high eastern plains. The peak was named for a hermit who supposedly lived in a cave near the summit.

If you parked in the lot at the entrance of the campground, the marked Trail 219 will be right across the road. It follows a beautiful, easy route far up El Porvenir Canyon. To find the Hermit Peak trail, walk along the road across the bridge into the campground. Across from the self-service pay station, a sign marks Trail 223 to Hermit Peak.

The trail immediately climbs out of the canyon onto a bench that slopes up toward Hermit Peak. The trail is well-used and easy to follow the entire way. At about 0.25 mile, the faint, but marked, Dispensas Trail forks to the right. Stay left toward Hermit Peak, as directed by the sign. At a little more than 0.5 mile, two old roads join the trail from the right, one after another. Stay left. About 100 feet after joining the roads, the marked trail to the peak climbs off to the right, leaving the roads.

The rocky trail climbs steadily, getting steeper as you progress. It crosses a small stream a couple of times in the first two miles. The next 1.5 miles switchback up a narrow canyon hemmed in by the peak's towering cliffs. This steep and rocky stretch is the hardest part of the hike. By the time that you hit the switchbacks, you have crossed the unmarked wilderness boundary.

Just as the steep switchbacks become interminable, you pop out onto a ridge at about 3.5 miles. The view is impressive. Right after reaching the top, the trail makes an unmarked fork. Take either fork; they quickly rejoin. A short distance up the trail lies Hermit Spring, enclosed in a steel and concrete box. A sign marks the water source. Blessedly, the last half mile to the summit

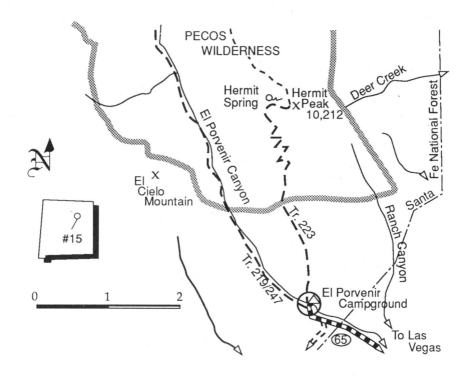

from the spring is on a much more level grade. The large wooded and relatively level summit that you will be crossing has numerous possible campsites. Wooden crosses have been erected along the way by a religious group.

At about four miles, a sign on the flat summit marks the continuation of Trail 223 to the left. It continues on to Lone Pine Mesa and Beaver Creek. About 100 yards straight ahead, visible from the sign, is the sheer eastern escarpment. Soak up the views far to the east; try to imagine the wagons of the Santa Fe Trail traversing the plains at the base of the mountains. Below you, the cliffs fall away hundreds of feet, producing vertigo in all but the least acrophobic.

Naturally, I arrived on the summit when it was wreathed in fog. It took some time for me to get much of a view. A sign near the rim marks the short trail to Hermit's Cave to the right (south). If you camp on the top, be sure to get up for the sunrise. A fourteen-mile loop can be made by continuing on Trail 223 and by turning left at every succeeding trail junction. Ultimately, you follow El Porvenir Canyon back down to the trailhead on combined Trail 219/247. The loop is best done as an overnight trip. El Porvenir Campground makes a beautiful base camp before or after your hike. It's usually quite busy on summer weekends.

HIKE 16 *TRAMPAS LAKES*

General description: A moderately strenuous day hike or overnight trip to two alpine lakes in the Pecos Wilderness.
General location: About forty miles south of Taos.
Length: About twelve miles round trip.
Elevation: 8,940-11,410 feet.
Maps: Pecos Wilderness, Carson National Forest, Truchas Peak and El Valle 7.5-minute USGS quads.
Best season: June through October.
Water availability: Rio de las Trampas.
Special attractions: High natural alpine lakes.
Finding the trailhead: Turn south onto NM 518 from NM 68 on the south side of Taos. Go about fifteen miles to the NM 75 junction. Turn right on NM 75 and go about 6.7 miles to the NM 76 junction. Go left on NM 76 4.4 miles to FR 207. The unmarked FR 207 junction is on the left. If you are coming north on NM 76 from Santa Fe and Chimayo, the FR 207 turnoff is 1.1 miles north of the little village of Trampas. Follow FR 207, a good all-weather gravel road, all the way to its end at the Trampas Trailhead Campground at 8.2 miles.

The hike: The northern end of the Pecos Wilderness is much less heavily visited than the areas around Santa Fe and the Pecos River drainage. When I did this hike on an August weekday I only encountered two other small groups. On summer weekends, the trail is probably moderately busy.

The two natural Trampas Lakes, and a third another mile up the trail, were formed when glaciers carved out basins in the rock and deposited rock dams, or moraines at the downstream ends of the basins. The lakes are tucked into forest just below timberline. Above tower sheer canyon walls and the 13,000-foot Truchas Peaks, the second highest in New Mexico.

The trailhead campground consists basically of a pit toilet and a sign but still makes a good camp before or after the hike. No water taps or tables are present. Creek water can be treated for use.

Trail 31, marked by a sign, climbs up the hill on the backside of the campground. The trail is one of the best designed and maintained that I have seen in the New Mexico mountains. Except for the last mile, the trail follows a very steady, moderate grade for the entire route up the Rio de las Trampas. Few rocks and roots lie on the smooth trail. Although the elevation gain and distance is considerable, the excellent trail makes the hike easier than it otherwise would be.

The trail follows the river the entire way, with a few easy crossings. An avalanche chute or two remind you that these are serious mountains. The best campsites are probably at about the three-mile point and at the lakes. The last mile does steepen considerably, with some rocky and muddy areas. At about six miles the trail forks. As marked by the sign, the Trampas Lakes are to the left and Hidden Lake is to the right. Go left toward the Trampas Lakes. Just a few feet up the left fork, a sign points the directions to the Upper and Lower Trampas Lakes. The upper lake is less than 100 yards to the right; the lower is a little farther to the left. The lower lake is larger, but both are beautiful. If you have time, be sure to hike the easy additional mile to Hidden Lake.

Cascades tumble down the Trampas River in the Pecos Wilderness.

The lakeshores have seen a lot of wear from hikers and campers. Camp well away from the lakes to try to minimize additional damage. Likewise, use good sanitation practices. Walk on already bare areas; try not to trample the fragile alpine vegetation.

HIKE 17 SAN LEONARDO LAKES

General description: A strenuous day hike or overnight trip to a pair of natural alpine lakes in the Pecos Wilderness.
General location: About forty miles south of Taos.
Length: About eight miles round trip.
Elevation: 9,340-11,360 feet.
Maps: Pecos Wilderness, Carson National Forest, El Valle 7.5-minute USGS quad.
Best season: June through October.
Water availability: San Leonardo Creek and Lakes.
Special attractions: High alpine lakes.
Finding the trailhead: Follow the same directions as those for Hike 16, Trampas Lakes. Instead of driving 8.2 miles up FR 207 to its end, go only 7.8 miles to the FR 639 turnoff. Go right, across the creek, on FR 639 for 1.3 miles. The trailhead, marked by a Trail 30 sign, is on the left where a small side road turns off. Unless you have a four-wheel drive, do not attempt to drive up FR 639 if it's wet or rain is threatening. Several spots can get very muddy and treacherous. Otherwise, with care, most vehicles should be able to make it up the road.

The hike: Although some maps show the lakes as only one lake, in reality there are two adjacent to each other. The northern end of the Pecos Wilderness is less visited than most of the wilderness in the Santa Fe area. Although these two lakes are probably among the least visited in the wilderness, they are no less scenic. Like the nearby Trampas Lakes (See Hike 16), they lie in a glacial cirque at timberline, surrounded by towering peaks.

From the sign at the side of FR 639, walk up the rough side road into the canyon formed by San Leonardo Creek. The little road can be driven for 0.3 mile by a high clearance vehicle if it's dry. At 0.3 mile the road is blocked and you must hike. The old road ends only another 0.1 mile or so along the way. From there, the remainder of the route is trail. Although the hike to the lakes is only about four miles, the trail is very steep and rocky, with numerous stream crossings. Even though the nearby Trampas Lakes Trail is longer and gains more altitude, this hike seemed harder to me. However, by being more difficult and a little more out of the way, this trail is only lightly used.

At a little more than 0.5 mile up from FR 639, you cross the marked Pecos Wilderness boundary. The trail follows the stream for the entire route. The crossings can be done with dry feet, but are tricky with a large pack. The trail passes through lush spruce and fir forest. The source of the stream is passed in a particularly steep stretch about three miles up. The water gushes out of a large spring right next to the trail.

Rain gear proves its value as clouds descend on Upper San Leonardo Lake in the Pecos Wilderness.

The trail finally levels out some for the last 0.25 mile before the lakes. As the trail crosses the little ridges left by the glaciers, it fades in and out. Just keep walking up toward the back of the valley, obvious now with its towering walls. You'll pass the smaller lower lake on the left and hit the second right afterwards at the very back of the valley.

The upper lake is a good-sized alpine lake, nestled into the steep slopes and cliffs of the cirque. A few patches of snow usually last through the summer at the base of the cliffs. Many dead tree trunks ring the shoreline, carried into the lake by a 1973 landslide.

As with all the alpine lakes, please don't camp on or near the shoreline and use good sanitary practices. The high elevation vegetation is very fragile. Unless you have to, it's best not to build campfires because of the shortage of firewood at the lakes' timberline location.

Be sure to take warm clothes and rain gear. It started raining on me within minutes of arriving at the lake and was still pouring two hours later when I got back to my car. I then slipped and slid back down FR 639, narrowly avoiding getting stuck.

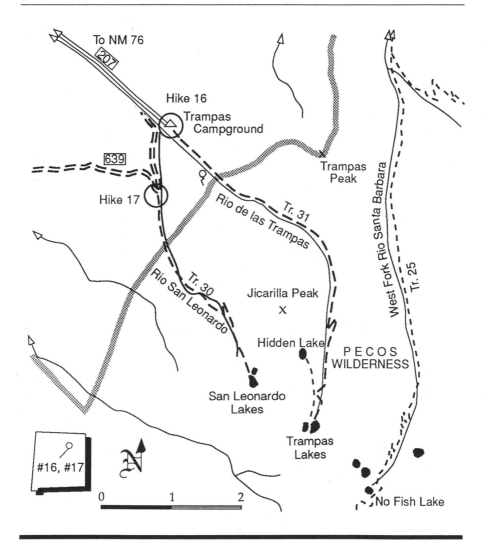

To NM 76

207

Hike 16

Trampas
Campground

639

Hike 17

Trampas
Peak

West Fork Rio Santa Barbara

Tr. 31

Rio de las Trampas

Tr. 30

Rio San Leonardo

Jicarilla Peak
X

Tr. 25

Hidden Lake

P E C O S
WILDERNESS

San Leonardo
Lakes

Trampas
Lakes

N

#16, #17

0   1   2

No Fish Lake

HIKE 18 *WHEELER PEAK*

General description: A very strenuous day hike or moderately strenuous two or three day trip to the summit of New Mexico's highest peak
General location: About twenty miles northeast of Taos
Length: About fifteen miles round trip
Elevation: 9,390-13,161 feet
Maps: Carson National Forest, Wheeler Peak 7.5-minute USGS quad
Best season: June through October
Water availability: Stream below summit ridge at about the five-mile point
Special attractions: Alpine terrain; tremendous views from New Mexico's highest peak
Finding the trailhead: Drive about 3.9 miles north of the center of Taos on NM 522 and turn right on NM 150. Follow this road about fifteen miles to Taos Ski Valley. Park in the upper gravel parking ramp at the end of the road across from the base of the ski area. Large Wheeler Peak Wilderness signs mark the trailhead.

The hike: Wheeler Peak lies in the center of the small 19,000-acre Wheeler Peak Wilderness. Several other of New Mexico's highest peaks lie in and around the wilderness. The peaks and ridges are one of the few areas in New Mexico with extensive amounts of alpine tundra vegetation. The glacial cirques on the slopes of the peaks contain many natural alpine lakes. Snowfields remain year round in patches.

Be sure to get a very early start on this hike. To minimize problems with storms, you ideally want to be on the summit before noon. Snow flurries are possible even in mid-summer. Be sure to take rain gear and extra warm clothing. Lightning and hypothermia are real threats on Wheeler Peak and the exposed summit ridge.

The heavily-used trail leads out of the parking area behind the trail signs and immediately begins climbing up the valley trending northeast. The first mile of the hike is extremely steep and rocky and, in my opinion, the hardest part of the entire hike. The first two miles to Bull-of-the-Woods Pasture are somewhat confusing. A maze of old roads and trails criss-cross with inadequate trail markings. However, the proper route is the most heavily worn and is easy to find. On a summer weekend, there will be plenty of people to follow. You won't get lost if you persist in following the valley northeast to Bull-of-the-Woods Pasture. The route stays fairly close to the stream in the valley bottom for the entire two miles.

At just short of one mile you will pass marked Trail 63, the Long Canyon Trail to Gold Hill, coming in from the left. Ignore it and continue climbing up the northeast-trending valley. Just past the trail junction, the trail hits an old road. Turn left onto the road and follow it the rest of the way up the valley. About a mile past Long Canyon the route levels out at Bull-of-the-Woods Pasture. The road forks at the edge of the level area. Turn right, following the sign toward Wheeler Peak.

The road quickly resumes climbing. The old road climbs up around the west side of Bull-of-the-Woods Mountain. A couple of old mines on the side and top of the peak are the destination of the old road. At about three miles the

Marmots inhabit alpine areas of the Sangre de Cristo Mountains, such as this spot by Williams Lake.

route leaves the old road and turns into an obvious trail. From here the trail is easy to follow all the way to the summit.

From this point on, most of the trail traverses the tundra above timberline. It follows the ridge south all the way to Wheeler Peak. If storms are building, do not venture beyond Bull-of-the-Woods Mountain, because the rest of the trail is very exposed to lightning. On my first attempt to climb Wheeler Peak, I was chased down the ridge from just short of the summit by a hair-raising lightning storm.

At about five miles, the trail drops slightly into a small forested valley, probably the only good camping area on the route, other than Bull-of-the-Woods Pasture. A small stream provides water in the valley bottom.

At about seven miles, the you reach the 13,133-foot summit of Mt. Walter (and you thought it was Wheeler Peak!). Don't despair, Wheeler Peak is less than 0.5 mile further. One hiker wrote in the register on Wheeler Peak:

Thought it was Wheeler,
And did not falter,
Was quite saddened,
To find it was Walter.

Enjoy the splendid views from the top of New Mexico. Ranks of snow-capped peaks line the horizon in Colorado. Alpine lakes fill the cirques at the base

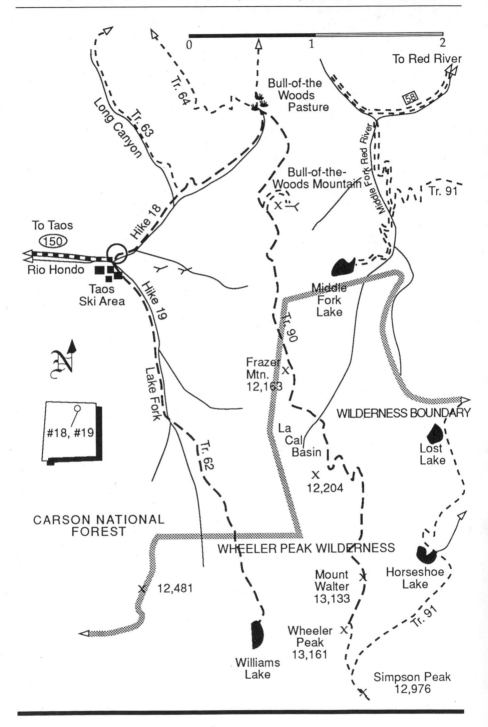

To Red River

Bull-of-the-Woods Pasture

58

Tr. 64

Tr. 63

Long Canyon

Middle Fork Red River

Bull-of-the-Woods Mountain

Tr. 91

Hike 18

To Taos

150

Rio Hondo

Taos Ski Area

Middle Fork Lake

Hike 19

Tr. 90

N

Lake Fork

Frazer Mtn. 12,163

#18, #19

La Cal Basin

WILDERNESS BOUNDARY

Lost Lake

Tr. 62

X 12,204

CARSON NATIONAL FOREST

WHEELER PEAK WILDERNESS

Horseshoe Lake

X 12,481

Mount Walter 13,133

Tr. 91

Wheeler Peak 13,161

Williams Lake

Simpson Peak 12,976

of the peak. Marmots look for handouts while the pikas harvest alpine grasses to last them through the long winter.

Unless you got a very early start, don't dawdle too long on the summit. Keep an eye out for storms, especially after lunch. They can build within minutes, threatening hikers with lightning, hail, rain, and cold. Remember, you have four miles of exposed ridge to cross on the way down. If the weather is particularly serious, consider dropping straight down the steep west side of the summit to Williams Lake. However, because hikers create serious erosion on the steep slope, I don't recommend the route except in emergencies.

HIKE 19 *WILLIAMS LAKE*

General description: A moderate hike to an alpine lake at the base of Wheeler Peak.

General location: About miles northeast of Taos.

Length: About eight miles round trip.

Elevation: 9,390-11,120 feet.

Maps: Carson National Forest, Wheeler Peak 7.5-minute USGS quad.

Best season: Mid-May through October.

Water availability: Lake Fork of Rio Hondo, stream feeding Williams Lake.

Special attractions: Natural alpine lake, lush forest.

Finding the trailhead: Follow same directions as Hike 18, Wheeler Peak.

The hike: Williams Lake nestles in a large glacial cirque at the western base of Wheeler Peak. The level of the small lake fluctuates somewhat, depending on precipitation. It doesn't support fish, possibly because the entire lake freezes some years due to its shallowness. High craggy peaks encircle the lake, providing a stunning setting.

Since the lake is easier to reach than most of the alpine lakes in New Mexico, the hike is popular on summer weekends. From the gravel ski area parking lot, cross the Rio Hondo on either the footbridge or road bridge into the heart of the ski village. Walk toward the two parallel chairlifts ascending the mountain behind the village. The first part of this hike is on private land, so please be courteous.

Climb up the hill underneath the two lifts a very short distance to the first ski trail that goes off into the woods to the left. Follow the ski trail for about 1.5 miles upstream, above the Lake Fork of the Rio Hondo, to the base of the Kachina Chairlift and the Phoenix restaurant. Cross the creek on the trail to the east side when you reach the lift and restaurant. Follow the dirt road up along the creek past the restaurant. The road forks about 100 yards upstream. The main road crosses the stream and climbs up the ski mountain. Stay left and follow the old road up the east side of the canyon. A sign at the road fork points the way to the lake.

The old road narrows to a trail in about 0.25 mile or so. The trail crosses the marked Wheeler Peak Wilderness boundary fairly soon afterwards. The trail climbs relatively steeply for the rest of the four miles to the large glacial basin containing Williams Lake. Along the way, you'll pass a couple of swaths

Williams Lake lies at the base of Wheeler Peak, New Mexico's highest point.

with flattened trees cut through the forest. Even in New Mexico, avalanches come blasting down from the high ridges in winter.

As with all alpine lakes, the vegetation around Williams Lake is very fragile. Since the lake is fairly heavily visited, camp well away from the shoreline and streams, ideally outside of the lake basin. Use a camp stove for cooking, instead of the scarce firewood. Return to the trailhead via the same route.

HIKE 20 *GOLD HILL*

General description: A strenuous day or overnight hike to a high peak above Red River and Taos Ski Valley.
General location: About twenty miles northeast of Taos.
Length: About ten miles round trip.
Elevation: 9,390-12,711 feet.
Maps: Carson National Forest, Wheeler Peak and Red River 7.5-minute USGS quads.
Best season: June through October.
Water availability: Long Canyon, Rio Hondo fork.
Special attractions: Spectacular views, tundra, bristlecone pines.
Finding the trailhead: Follow the same directions as Hike 18, Wheeler Peak.

The hike: The name Gold Hill is somewhat misleading, since the peak is one of the highest summits in northern New Mexico. Since the peak is separated by several miles from any other summits of comparable height, Gold Hill commands tremendous views of the northern New Mexico mountains. The peak provides views almost as spectacular as Wheeler Peak, New Mexico's highest, but has far fewer people. If you arrive at the trailhead parking lot and find a traffic jam, consider climbing Gold Hill rather than Wheeler Peak (See Hike 18).

Be sure to get an early start on this hike. To avoid thunderstorms, you want to be on the summit before noon. Snow flurries are possible even in mid-summer. Be sure to take rain gear and extra warm clothing. Lightning and hypothermia are real threats on the summit and areas above timberline.

The first two miles follow the same route as the Wheeler Peak Trail. The heavily-used trail leads out of the parking area behind the trail signs and immediately begins climbing up the valley trending northeast. The first mile of the hike is extremely steep and rocky and, in my opinion, the hardest part of the entire hike. The first two miles to Bull-of-the-Woods Pasture are somewhat confusing. A maze of old roads and trails criss-cross with inadequate trail markings. However, the proper route is the most heavily worn and is easy to find. On a summer weekend, there will be plenty of people to follow. You won't get lost if you persist in following the valley northeast to Bull-of-the-Woods Pasture. The route stays fairly close to the Rio Hondo in the valley bottom for the entire two miles.

At just short of one mile you will pass marked Trail 63, the Long Canyon Trail to Gold Hill, coming in from the left. This will be your return route coming down from Gold Hill. Ignore it for now and continue climbing up the northeast-trending valley. Just past the trail junction, the trail hits an old road. Turn left onto the road and follow it the rest of the way up the valley. About a mile past Long Canyon the route levels out at Bull-of-the-Woods Pasture.

The area is well named. Sure enough, I ran into a large bull and a herd of cows on the old road just short of the pasture. Fortunately, they were more interested in grazing than in me. The road forks at the edge of the pasture. Turn left at the fork, off of the Wheeler Peak route, go about fifty feet along

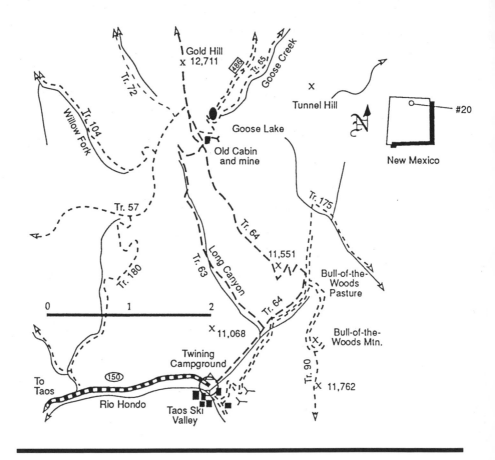

the old road, and turn left again off the road onto the Gold Hill trail. A sign marks the turnoff.

The trail climbs steeply up onto a wooded ridge above the pasture. The trail levels out and even goes slightly downhill for about 0.5 mile, giving a good breather after the steep first half of the hike. The trail then pops out of the dense spruce forest onto a bare area that gives great views of Taos Ski Valley to the south. The breather ends and the trail resumes climbing.

At a little over four miles, at timberline, the trail encounters an old mine and ruined cabin. Actually, the official trail to Gold Hill forks left just before the cabin, but it's easy to miss. So just go on up to the cabin and climb to the summit from there.

By now you should be puffing and panting in the thin air. Relax and enjoy the views from the cabin before the final push. While you're resting, look carefully about 100 yards across the meadow to the west and you'll see a sign marking the Long Canyon trail. Note carefully where it is in relation to the cabin, since that will be your return route. The trail gets somewhat faint on the flower-covered tundra above timberline. The trail to Long Canyon is generally easier to find on the way down.

From the cabin, follow the faint trail up onto the top of the bare ridge just above. At this point the trail fades out. However, just walk up the ridge to the left to the obvious summit. Part way up the ridge the official trail reappears from the left. Goose Lake will be visible far below to your right. Ignore the steep Goose Lake Trail 65 that drops down to it. Follow the last stretch of trail up to the rounded summit, passing the marked turnoff to Lobo Peak that goes downhill to the left.

Relax and enjoy the incredible views. Numerous 13- and 14,000-foot peaks line the horizon to the north in Colorado. The closer Latir Peaks of New Mexico lie across the Red River canyon to the north. Several miles to the south towers Wheeler Peak. Keep an eye out for storms building. Be ready to flee at the first sign.

The trail continues on down the other side of the summit, eventually winding up in either Columbine Campground or the town of Red River. A car shuttle would make such a hike feasible. If you have time and the weather permits, consider hiking out along the alpine ridges on the Lobo Peak Trail.

For the return, try the Long Canyon Trail. It's similar in length and difficulty. Retrace your route back down the summit ridge to the Lobo Peak sign. The trail gets faint here, but keep going the same direction downwards through the open tundra to the Goose Lake junction sign. Pass that sign and keep going the same direction downwards. The trail is faint but visible. In a few hundred yards you'll hit the Long Canyon sign, the same sign that you saw from the old miner's cabin 100 yards away. The Long Canyon trail goes straight southwest from the sign, as indicated by the arrow, to the edge of Long Canyon a couple of hundred yards distant. Some wood posts and rock cairns mark the route. At the canyon rim, the trail becomes well-worn and obvious for the rest of the return. If you have trouble finding the route to Long Canyon, just go back to the miner's cabin and return via the way that you came up.

A lot of gnarled bristlecone pines line the first few hundred yards of the trail as you drop down into Long Canyon. I also saw large patches of Colorado blue columbine on the slope. The trail drops steadily down the canyon, encountering the creek after a while. It finally rejoins the trail to Bull-of-the-Woods Pasture. Turn right and walk down the last steep mile.

The best campsites are probably at Bull-of-the-Woods Pasture, the level ridgetop above the pasture, and especially in the scattered forest just below the miner's cabin and in upper Long Canyon.

HIKE 21 *EAST FORK RED RIVER*

General description: A relatively easy hike to the edge of the Wheeler Peak Wilderness.

General location: About seven miles south of Red River.

Length: About 6.5 miles round trip.

Elevation: 9,640-10,800 feet.

Maps: Carson National Forest, Wheeler Peak 7.5-minute USGS quad.

Best season: May through October.

Water availability: East Fork Red River, Sawmill Creek.

Special attractions: Lush forest, mountain streams.

Finding the trailhead: From Red River, take NM 578 south 6.2 miles to the marked turnoff to the East Fork of the Red River. Go left across the bridge at the end of the pavement, as directed by the sign. The road splits several ways after crossing the bridge. Turn right, following the broad, rocky road up the hill. Ignore the driveways on the right. Follow the road south 1.25 miles to the marked trailhead, past numerous summer homes. The road is marked

The trail up the East Fork of the Red River crosses into the Wheeler Peak Wilderness.

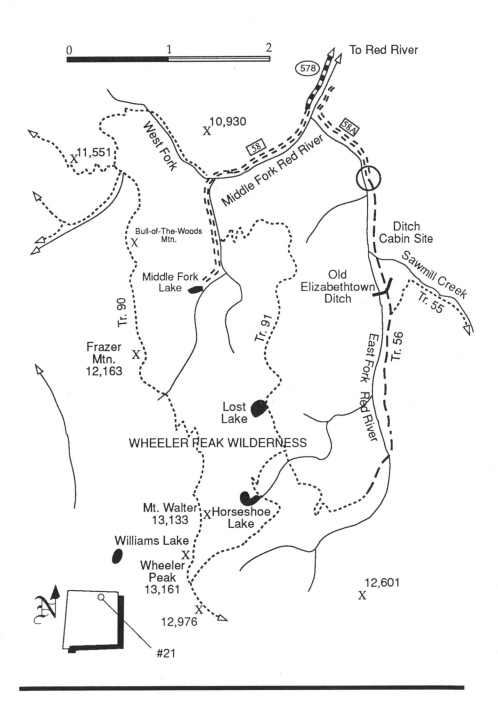

0   1   2

To Red River

578

West Fork

X 10,930

58

X 11,551

58A

Middle Fork Red River

Ditch
Cabin Site

Bull-of-The-Woods
Mtn.
X

Sawmill Creek

Middle Fork
Lake

Old
Elizabethtown
Ditch

Tr. 55

Tr. 90

Tr. 91

East Fork Red River

Tr. 56

Frazer
Mtn.
12,163
X

Lost
Lake

WHEELER PEAK WILDERNESS

Mt. Walter
13,133
X Horseshoe
Lake

Williams Lake

X

Wheeler
Peak
13,161

12,601
X

X
12,976

#21

FR 58 on the ground, FR 58-A on the old Carson National Forest map, and FR 54-A on the new map, so take your pick. When dry, the rocky road should be passable to most vehicles if care is used. When wet, a muddy spot about halfway along can be treacherous to vehicles other than four-wheel drives. Walking part of the road will not add much to the hike.

The hike: The mountains around the Taos and Red River area are the highest in the state, with many high peaks and alpine lakes. The high elevations create some of the most spectacular hikes in this book but require a considerable amount of climbing, making them moderate to strenuous in difficulty. This hike, up the lush East Fork of the Red River, is a relatively easy hike through dense forest to the edge of the Wheeler Peak Wilderness. The Red River is a major Rio Grande tributary.

From the marked trailhead at the end of the road, hike up the hill behind the trail signs and follow the old road, now made impassable to vehicles. Trail 56 climbs through thick spruce and fir, reaching a clearing at the Ditch Cabin Site in a little less than 0.75 mile. The old road ends at the site and the trail continues onward, crossing Sawmill Creek. The trail climbs upstream, high on the wooded slope above the East Fork. At about 1.25 miles, you reach the old Elizabethtown Ditch. The forty-one mile-long ditch carried water from the East Fork to gold mines in the Moreno Valley. The abandoned ditch was built in 1868 by Lucien Maxwell. With some bushwhacking, the ditch can be followed for miles.

At about 1.5 miles, the Sawmill Park Trail 55 climbs up to the left. Stay right, following the sign to Lost Lake. At about 2.75 miles, the trail crosses to the right, or west, side of the East Fork on a sturdy wooden bridge. A half mile climb up the west bank from the river brings you to the marked Wheeler Peak Wilderness boundary, just after crossing a small side creek.

Return to the trailhead by the same route, or continue as far as energy and desire take you. Horseshoe and Lost Lakes are about three miles farther up the trail. A fourteen-mile loop can be done by following Trail 91 past Lost Lake and down the Middle Fork of the Red River to FR 58. Go down FR 58 to NM 578 and walk the 1.25 miles back up FR 58-A to the trailhead.

HIKE 22 *RIO GRANDE GORGE*

General description: A relatively easy hike down into the rocky canyon of the Rio Grande Wild and Scenic River.
General location: About thirty-five miles northwest of Taos.
Length: About seven miles round trip.
Elevation: 7,450-6560 feet.
Maps: Wild Rivers Recreation Area BLM brochure, Guadalupe Mountain 7.5-minute USGS quad.
Best season: Year round.
Water availability: Trailhead, Big and Little Arsenic Springs.
Special attractions: Rugged canyon of the Rio Grande.
Finding the trailhead: From the center of Questa (about twenty miles north of Taos), drive north on NM 522 about 2.6 miles to the marked turnoff to the the Rio Grande Wild and Scenic River (NM 378). Turn left (west) and drive 11.7 miles on the paved road to the marked Big Arsenic Springs Campground entrance. Drive into the campground, taking either of the two forks encountered just after leaving NM 378. The marked trailhead is located at the back of the campground on the canyon rim. Unless you pay the overnight camping fee, be sure not to park at a campsite. The campground, along with several others along the canyon rim, makes an excellent place to spend the night. The campgrounds, with water, tables, and pit toilets, rarely fill up, even in summer.

The hike: The rugged canyon of the Rio Grande, from the Colorado border south for forty-eight miles, was protected by Congress as a National Wild and Scenic River. The protected area includes the Red River from its confluence to a point four miles upstream.

Over millions of years, the Rio Grande has carved a deep canyon through the relatively flat plains on the west side of the Sangre de Cristo Mountains. The canyon rim falls off abruptly in a series of sheer basalt cliffs. The narrow canyon is over 800 feet deep in the area of the hike.

The canyon is suitable for hiking all year. Summers can be quite hot, making the climb out of the canyon fairly strenuous. The occasional winter snows usually melt off fairly quickly. Although nearby Taos and Red River may be crowded with tourists in summer and skiers in winter, the Wild Rivers Recreation Area is surprisingly undiscovered. The campgrounds along the rim were only half full when I last visited on a summer Friday evening. Most of the hikes in northern New Mexico are mountain hikes. This trail makes an interesting change.

From the trailhead on the rim, the trail drops steeply down well-maintained switchbacks into the canyon. The rim is wooded with pinyon pine and juniper. As you descend into the canyon, you encounter ponderosa pine on the slopes and along the river. Usually ponderosa pine grows at higher elevations than pinyon and juniper, but apparently the canyon walls provide enough extra protection for ponderosa to grow.

At about 0.6 mile, the trail forks. Go right, toward Big Arsenic Springs, as marked. The trail goes 0.4 mile, passing several three-sided metal camping shelters along the river. The large springs gush out of the base of a talus slope

Scattered ponderosa pines line the rocky gorge of the Rio Grande.

and pass under the trail before flowing into the river. The Rio Grande here is not the slow muddy river of most of New Mexico. It roars and tumbles downstream, around boulders and over cascades.

The shelters make excellent sites for an overnight stay. They rarely fill up because of the hike required to reach them. Fishermen sometimes use them as camps. Retrace the 0.4 mile back up to the trail junction and continue downstream along the river, toward La Junta. About a mile down the river from the junction, the trail passes the smaller Little Arsenic Springs and a camp shelter. A little less than 0.25 mile further is another junction. The left fork climbs 0.8 mile back up to the rim at Little Arsenic Springs Campground. Stay right, down the river toward La Junta. Just past the junction lie several more camping shelters tucked into a stand of ponderosa pine.

About 2.1 miles from the first junction (Big Arsenic Springs), the trail hits the third fork. The left fork climbs up to La Junta Campground on the rim. Go downstream to the right, to La Junta at the confluence of the Red River and Rio Grande. More camping shelters provide fine campsites. From here several options are possible for the return trip, all of relatively similar length and difficulty. You can retrace the same trail all the way back or climb out the trails to Little Arsenic Springs or La Junta campgrounds. From the two campgrounds, just follow the road back to the trailhead at Big Arsenic Springs Campground.

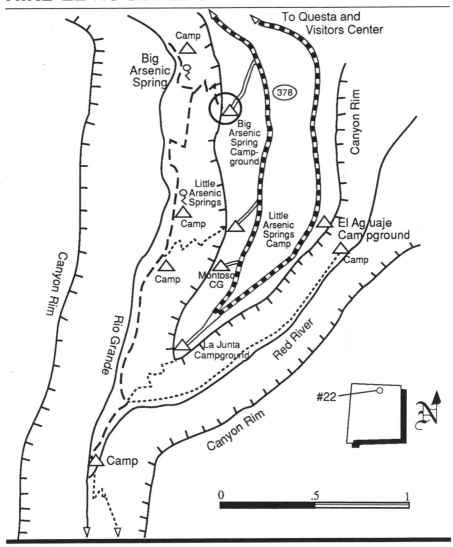

The hike can be lengthened a mile by crossing the Red River footbridge next to the shelters at La Junta. The trail follows down the river and then climbs up to Cebolla Mesa Campground on the rim. Another option involves following the unmaintained trail upstream on the bank of the Red River for about two miles to the formal trail that comes down from El Aguaje Campground on the rim. Several other shorter loops are possible using different combinations of the trails.

General description: An easy day hike in the remote Peloncillo Mountains of far southwestern New Mexico.

General location: About forty miles south of Animas in the Coronado National Forest.

Length: About five miles round trip.

Elevation: 5,450-6,000 feet.

Maps: Coronado National Forest, Animas Peak and Cienega Springs 15-minute USGS quads.

Best season: All year.

Water availability: Seasonal at Blackwater Hole.

Special attractions: Solitude; Chihuahua pines; birds.

Finding the trailhead: Take State Highway 338 south from Animas about thirty miles (pavement ends after twenty miles) and turn at the marked junction to Douglas, Arizona. Follow the unpaved Douglas road west without turning at any junctions to the Coronado National Forest Boundary. Go two miles further to a small left fork that climbs up the bank. Drive up the fork fifty yards to an open area and park. The fork is rough; those without a high-clearance vehicle may want to park along the main road. The rest of the dirt roads are good, except during and after heavy rains, which usually occur in late summer.

The hike: The far southwestern corner of New Mexico, the "Bootheel," is one of the least visited areas of the state. At the nearby Port of Entry on the Mexican border at Antelope Wells, only four vehicles per day enter the U.S. To the surprise of first-time visitors, the southern part of the Bootheel consists of lush grasslands and partially wooded mountains.

The Peloncillo Mountains straddle the Arizona-New Mexico line, continuing south into Mexico. Successive ranges farther south lead into the remote Sierra Madre. The Peloncillos consist of low rounded hills, covered with grass and scattered oaks, pinyon pines, and junipers, leading into a more rugged crest with peaks reaching 6,500 feet in elevation.

The hike follows up a fork of Clanton Draw to a relatively permanent pool called Blackwater Hole and up to the site of an old corral. Clanton Draw was named for the hideout of the Clanton Gang, notorious for their shootout at the OK Corral in Tombstone, Arizona. The Clantons used the hideout, only a mile or so from the trailhead, to raid Mexican smuggler parties in the 1880s. Nearby Skeleton Canyon was named for the many bones left after two particularly brutal raids in 1881.

The first part of the hike follows an old jeep trail up the canyon for about one-half mile. The canyon sometimes flows in late summer and fall after the rainy season. After the road disappears, the trail becomes very faint from disuse. You can follow the canyon bottom the rest of the way, but the remnants of the old trail cross the dry creek bottom back and forth to the benches lining the creek. If you can stay with the old trail, it's generally easier to walk on the benches. Several small side canyons will join the canyon. Stay in the main canyon which, although it winds some, trends southwest the entire route to Blackwater Hole.

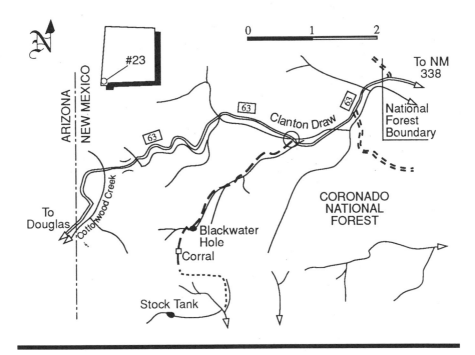

As you hike, you'll pass through small groves of Chihuahua pines. The only place that the tree grows in the U.S. is in a few of the mountain ranges of New Mexico's Bootheel and adjoining areas of Arizona. It looks similar to the Ponderosa pine, but with shorter needles and darker colored bark.

You reach Blackwater Hole, a pond created by a small concrete dam, at about two miles. Because the pond is basically a cattle tank, carrying your own water is recommended. About 200-300 yards upstream from the pond, a small drainage climbs steeply to the left. The faint trail climbs up out of the main canyon on the west side of the small draw. Shortly after you climb out of the canyon, you reach the end of the hike at a large grassy meadow, site of an old corral. The meadow, spotted with junipers, makes a good campsite. A short walk up the hill to the south of the meadow gives great views of the Animas Mountains to the east and the San Luis Mountains of Mexico to the southeast. The Forest Service map indicates a trail leading south from the corral, but it's difficult to follow. Following the rounded ridge tops with a map and compass is the easiest way to lengthen the trip.

Keep an eye out for birds on the hike. The mountains are famous among birders, especially at the southern end of the range in Guadalupe Canyon. The proximity to Mexico gives the Peloncillos one of the largest numbers of bird species in the United States.

Be sure to take maps and a compass with you on hikes in the Peloncillos. Trails are faint to nonexistent and you are very unlikely to see anyone else during your hikes.

HIKE 24 *CAPULIN VOLCANO*

General description: A very easy hike with spectacular views from the crater rim of a recent volcano.
General location: About thirty miles east of Raton.
Length: One-mile loop.
Elevation: 7,880-8,182 feet.
Maps: Folsom 7.5-minute USGS quad.
Best season: Spring through fall.
Water availability: none.
Special attractions: large symmetrical volcanic crater; tremendous views.
Finding the trailhead: From park headquarters at Capulin Volcano National Monument, take the two-mile road that spirals up to the parking lot on the crater rim.

The hike: Ten thousand years ago, Capulin Volcano built up over a thousand feet above the surrounding plain by fountains of ash and lava. Scores of other surrounding peaks and hills were built during the same period of volcanism. Because Capulin's three lava flows erupted from vents at the base of the mountain, the peak retained a very symmetrical cone shape. In the center of the cone lies the original sunken crater.

The loop trail begins and ends at the parking lot. The climb is less steep if you start on the south side. The trail follows the circular rim of the crater. Even though the crater is relatively new, vegetation has gained a good foothold on the steep, cinder-covered mountain. The trail passes through windswept stands of pinyon pine and juniper. Mountain mahogany, squawbush, gambel oak, and chokecherry form shrubby thickets. Open areas are heavily vegetated by grasses.

The trail affords continuous 360-degree views of the surrounding plains and mountains. Scattered volcanic hills and mountains break up the endless expanse of lush grasslands. Ten miles to the southeast lies Sierra Grande, the largest of the volcanos. To the west tower the snow-capped peaks of the Sangre de Cristo Mountains. On a clear day you can see the highest point in Oklahoma, Black Mesa, far to the east.

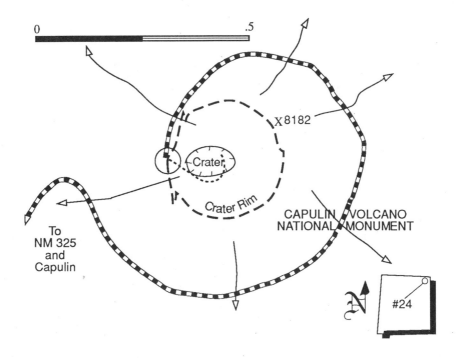

0   .5

X 8182

Crater

Crater Rim

CAPULIN VOLCANO
NATIONAL MONUMENT

To
NM 325
and
Capulin

#24

HIKE 25 _ANGEL PEAK_

General description: A moderate hike into the badlands below Angel Peak.
General location: About thirty-four miles southeast of Farmington.
Length: About two miles round trip.
Elevation: 6,680 to 6,250 feet.
Maps: East Fork Kutz Canyon and Huerfanito Peak 7.5-minute USGS quads.
Best season: Year round.
Water availability: None.
Special attractions: Colorful eroded badlands.
Finding the trailhead: From the intersection of US 64 and NM 44 in Bloomfield, drive south about fifteen miles on US 44. Turn left, northeast, onto a gravel road marked with a BLM Angel Peak Recreation Area sign. The road is good, but has some washboard. Initially the road crosses sagebrush flats, but quickly reaches the steep rim of the canyons below. Be sure to stop at some of the overlooks. Park at Angel Peak Campground at the end of the main gravel road, a little less than 6.5 miles from NM 44.

The hike: The route leads down into the badlands below the canyon rim on the north side of the campground. There are no formal trails. Since the route is steep and several sandstone ledges must be worked around, the hike isn't recommended for inexperienced hikers or children alone.

The colorful badlands were cut by drainages flowing into the San Juan River about ten or fifteen miles north. Angel Peak is the prominent peak about a mile north of the campground. The clay and sandstone beds exposed in the badlands are but a small part of the huge sedimentary San Juan Basin. Deeply buried sandstone layers form one of the largest natural gas fields in the United States. Widely scattered gas wells, visible from the hike, reduce the area's wildness, but don't seriously harm the badlands' scenic beauty.

Follow the canyon rim on the northeast side of the campground to the northeast about 0.25 mile until you reach a long ridge sloping downward to the west. Hike down the ridgetop into the badlands, scrambling down the occasional sandstone ledges. In about one-half mile the ridge peters out into a broad sandy wash at the bottom. A short walk farther down the wash brings you to the oilfield road that goes down the middle of the canyon. Picnic shelters of the campground will visible on the rim above for the entire hike. Return via the same route or bushwhack up one of the other many ridges that climb up to the rim.

The Angel Peak area can be very cold in winter and hot in summer, but generally the hike is good any time of year. Right after a heavy rain or snow, the clay soil gets very slick and muddy, making the hike difficult. The free BLM campground, set among the gnarled junipers clinging to the canyon rim, has pit toilets, picnic tables, and shelters. Be sure to at least stay until dark to watch the last rays of the sun turn the badlands flaming shades of red and gold.

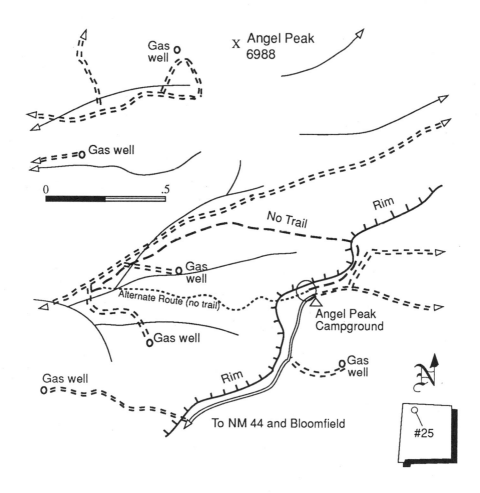

Gas well

X Angel Peak
6988

Gas well

0   .5

No Trail

Rim

Gas well

Alternate Route (no trail)

Angel Peak
Campground

Gas well

Gas well

Gas well

Rim

N

#25

To NM 44 and Bloomfield

HIKE 26 *BISTI BADLANDS*

General description: An easy hike into the tortured badlands of the Bisti Wilderness.
General location: About thirty miles south of Farmington.
Length: Four miles round trip.
Elevation: 5,770-5,850 feet.
Maps: Bisti Trading Post and Alamo Mesa West 7.5-minute USGS quads.
Best season: Spring and fall.
Water availability: None.
Special attractions: Colorful eroded badlands with pinnacles, hoodoos, and many other features.
Finding the trailhead: Drive about 25.5 miles south of Farmington on NM 371 (from the NM 371 intersection with US 64 on the south side of downtown Farmington). Turn left onto a good gravel road that runs almost parallel to the highway, but angles slightly southeast. Be sure not to turn left onto the gravel road that turns off only about 0.3 mile north of the proper road (it angles northeast). Follow the gravel road about three miles to the parking area on the left side of the road. The parking lot lies just past the Gateway Coal Mine entrance and is well marked with a BLM wilderness sign.

The hike: The Bisti Wilderness contains a maze of eroded clay beds and sandstone remnants. The clay beds, colored many shades of gray, with highlights of red and yellow, are very soft and erode easily. Little vegetation grows on the poor, unstable soil. Remnants of a harder sandstone caprock protect the softer underlying clay beds, producing many fanciful forms, from mushroom-shaped formations to pinnacles and small arches. The soft sedimentary beds also contain many seams of coal, obvious as black bands on eroded hillsides. Many of the coal seams are thick enough to make mining economic all over the Farmington area. The Bisti Wilderness contains considerable coal, but fortunately the area was preserved as wilderness because of its unique badlands.

This trail description is meant only as an introduction to the Bisti Badlands. No trails really exist in the wilderness. The badlands can seem maze-like to the inexperienced hiker, making it easy to get lost. However, if you're a beginner, don't be afraid to at least walk into the edge of the badlands. To go farther, take a map and compass and go with experienced hikers.

From the parking lot, a faint broad trail leads east along the fence marking the boundary of the Gateway Mine to the north. The trail fades out at about one-half mile. Continue to follow the coal mine fence until it turns north in about another one-quarter mile. From the fence corner, continue east-northeast up the broad low-relief wash. Mushroom rocks and hoodoos will be encountered soon after leaving the mine area. Keeping the mine in view will help prevent getting lost. I show the hike as going another 1.25 miles past the mine, but there really is no defined length. Wander at will among the weird rock formations, but be careful to keep track of direction. If you get lost, just hike west until you hit the mine, the gravel road, or NM 371.

The Bisti is good for hiking anytime of year. Summers can be very hot, however, with little shade. Winters are generally good, but the occasional snow

Shiprock is a prominent landmark northwest of the Bisti Badlands.

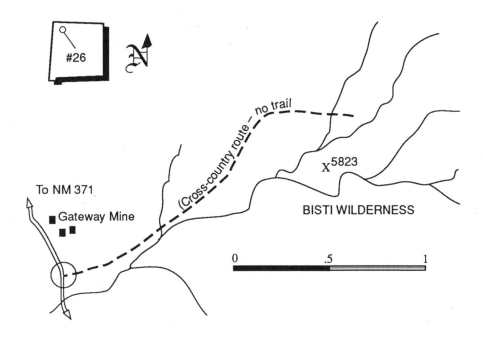

storm can make for a frigid hike. A friend and I hiked in the Bisti in February on a day with a low, threatening sky. About a mile from the car, a snow squall hit, instantly cutting visibility to a few hundred feet. We hustled back before we got lost. By next morning the badlands had received six inches of snow.

HIKE 27 *PUEBLO ALTO*

General description: An easy hike to several Anasazi ruins in Chaco Culture National Historical Park.

General location: About seventy miles south of Farmington.

Length: About five miles round trip.

Elevation: 6,140-6,435 feet.

Maps: National Park Service map and brochure, Pueblo Bonito 7.5-minute USGS quad.

Best season: All year.

Water availability: None.

Special attractions: Isolation; Anasazi ruins.

Finding the trailhead: Follow the same directions as for Hike 28, Penasco Blanco. Continue less than a mile further into the park from Casa Chiquita and stop at the parking lot for Kin Kletso ruin.

Kin Kletso ruin lies covered with snow at the start of the Pueblo Alto Trail.

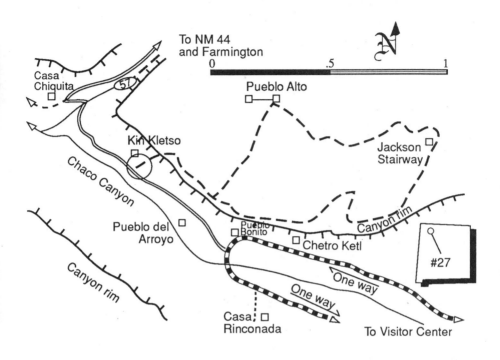

The hike: The many ruins in and surrounding Chaco Canyon were the center of the Anasazi civilization in northwestern New Mexico. From about 900 to 1200 AD, towns and villages flourished. Today only the crumbling ruins remain, abandoned for uncertain reasons. Archaeologists suspect that a combination of drought and abuse of the local environment led to disintegration of the culture.

Be sure to walk around Kin Kletso before starting up the trail. The large, but compact ruin had about 100 rooms and may have risen three stories. The Pueblo Alto trail starts from the back side of Kin Kletso and immediately scrambles up through a narrow cleft in the canyon wall. The trail winds to the southeast along the canyon rim, giving excellent views of Kin Kletso and Pueblo del Arroyo below. The trail often crosses bare slickrock, but is well marked with rock cairns. At a little less than a mile from the start, the trail forks. Stay right and continue along the canyon rim. At the fork, be sure to walk out onto the sandstone promontory to look down at the massive Pueblo Bonito ruin below. With 600 rooms and forty kivas, the four story pueblo is the largest in the park.

Farther along the rim, the trail overlooks 500-room Chetro Ketl ruin. Beyond Chetro Ketl, the trail contours around a side canyon, at one point following a section of prehistoric road. The trail then gradually climbs northeast toward the crest of the mesa. Near the top of the mesa, the trail overlooks an Anasazi stairway, the Jackson Stairs, climbing out of a side canyon. From the stairs, the trail follows the mesa top west for about a mile to Pueblo Alto, overlooking ancient farming terraces on the way.

Pueblo Alto, at the very crest of the mesa, is divided into two sections. The trail reaches the larger ruin, Old Alto, first. Old Alto has deteriorated more than its sister ruin, New Alto, located a few hundred yards farther west. Enjoy the view from the ruins. For miles and miles in every direction stretch nothing but empty sagebrush flats, cut by the occasional canyon. The vast country dwarfs even the elaborate ruins of Chaco Canyon.

From Pueblo Alto, the trails slowly drops back down toward Chaco Canyon to the southwest. The loop trail ends at the junction at the Pueblo Bonito overlook. From there, follow the same trail back to Kin Kletso and the trailhead. For those with limited time, follow the left fork at the overlook straight up to Pueblo Alto. The round trip is reduced to three miles by cutting off the loop.

HIKE 28 *PENASCO BLANCO*

General description: An easy day hike to a major Anasazi ruin in Chaco Culture National Historical Park.

General location: About seventy miles south of Farmington.

Length: 4.2 miles round trip.

Elevation: 6,110-6,270 feet.

Maps: National Park Service map and brochure, Pueblo Bonito and Kin Klizhin 7.5-minute USGS quads.

Best season: All year.

Water availability: None.

Special attractions: Large Anasazi ruin; isolation.

Finding the trailhead: Drive south of Bloomfield on NM 44 about twenty-eight miles to the Blanco Trading Post. Turn right (southwest) on dirt NM 57. Signs for Chaco Culture National Historical Park mark the turnoff. Drive about twenty-six miles to the park. A short distance after the park boundary, the road drops abruptly into Chaco Canyon. Casa Chiquita is on the right, immediately after the road reaches the canyon bottom. The trailhead is at the parking lot for Casa Chiquita ruin. In rainy or snowy weather, the long clay-surfaced dirt road can be treacherous, if not impassable. When dry, the road is notorious for its washboard surface. Bear with it; it keeps the crowds away. The park can also be approached on similar roads from Crownpoint to the south.

The hike: Chaco Canyon was a major center for the widespread Anasazi civilization of the Southwest. Extensive masonry ruins dot the canyon floors and surrounding mesas. The largest, Pueblo Bonito, had 600 rooms and forty kivas. The villages thrived for two hundred years, but were abandoned in the late AD 1100s. Why did the inhabitants leave? A prolonged drought and human degradation of the environment appear to be likely causes. Today only the lonesome wind inhabits the tumbling sandstone walls.

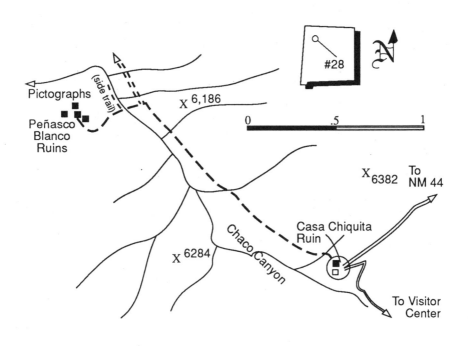

From the parking lot, the trail follows an abandoned dirt road northwest down the broad sandy Chaco Canyon floor. Keep an eye on the nearby north wall of the canyon. In several spots, ancient petroglyphs adorn the buff-colored sandstone. Unfortunately, more recent visitors have sometimes added their graffiti. After following the canyon bottom for about 1.5 miles, the old road forks. The right fork, faint and little-used continues down the canyon. Take the more-travelled left fork and cross the creek bottom. Before reaching the south wall of the canyon, a side trail takes off to the right. It goes a few hundred yards to visit some pictographs painted on the walls and roof of an overhang. One painting, on the roof of the overhang, is thought to represent the supernova of 1054 AD.

The main trail winds its way up the sandstone ledges of the south wall to Penasco Blanco ruin, perched on a point of the mesa that forms the canyon wall. The ruin isn't as well- preserved as some of the ruins in the canyon, but many walls still stand. Please don't climb on the fragile walls or collect artifacts.

From the ruin, you can see far up and down the canyon. Few people make the hike, so you'll probably have the ruin to yourself. I visited Penasco Blanco in February after a heavy snowfall. I reached the ruin shortly before sunset, after breaking trail through the snow. The mercury was falling as fast as the sun sank in the west. Combined with a wind howling out of the northwest across the treeless mesas, my sense of cold and isolation was extreme. It was hard to picture the ruins ever being inhabited.

HIKE 29 *MOUNT TAYLOR*

General description: A moderately strenuous dayhike to the summit of an extinct volcano.
General location: About twenty miles northeast of Grants.
Length: About six miles round trip.
Elevation: 9,280-11,301 feet.
Maps: Cibola National Forest—Mt. Taylor Ranger District, Mount Taylor, Cerro Pelon, San Mateo, and Lobo Springs 7.5-minute USGS quads.
Best season: May through October.
Water availability: Gooseberry Spring—see text.
Special attractions: Views, solitude.
Finding the trailhead: From the center of Grants, take NM 547 northeast toward the mountain. The route out of town is well-marked with Mount Taylor and route signs. Follow NM 547 for 13.3 miles to the FR 193 turnoff at the end of the pavement. Turn right on improved gravel road FR 193 and go 5.1 miles to the trailhead (only about 0.1 mile short of the FR 501 turnoff). The trailhead, on the left side of the road, is marked by Trail 77 signs.

The hike: Several million years ago, Mount Taylor erupted, creating a large volcano in the midst of an extensive plateau capped by several hundred feet of basalt. Numerous volcanic necks and cinder cones surround the main volcano. To the south, at El Malpais National Monument, lava flowed as recently as 1,000 years ago. Today, dense forests of pine, fir, aspen, and spruce cloak the old volcano's slopes. The solitary towering peak, snowcapped much of the year, forms one of the most prominent landmarks of northwestern New Mexico.

Unfortunately, even though Mount Taylor is such a major peak, the trail to the summit appears to be the only significant trail in the entire mountain range. The trail starts in mixed ponderosa and aspen forest, and begins climbing at an easy to moderate grade immediately. The first part of the trail appears to be new and has been rerouted from the old trailhead. Since the trail is new and little-used, it can be faint at times. Look closely and you should have no trouble finding it.

At a little over 0.5 mile, the trail drops down into the draw that it has been paralleling from the start. An old road (probably the old trail) joins the draw from the other side. A sign with motor vehicle restrictions marks the spot. A small seasonal spring sometimes flows here. Walk up the broad, open draw past the sign. The trail up the draw is basically a faint old road. At a little over a mile, the road passes a metal stock watering tank. The tank probably is fed by Gooseberry Spring, but I didn't see any water on my visit. Check with the Forest Service about the spring's status ahead of time.

Just past the tank, another sign restricts motor vehicles. Just past the sign, the obvious trail climbs straight up the right bank of the draw. Follow the

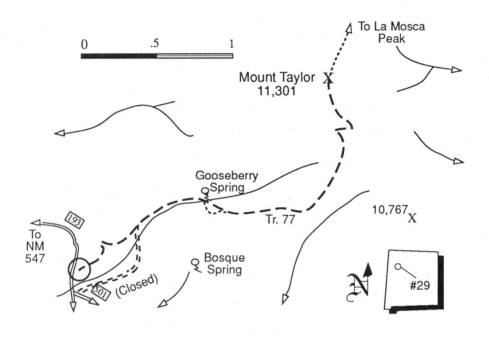

steep route and turn left onto the trail just short of the top. The trail quickly leaves the forest and comes out onto the steep grassy slopes of the mountain. The summit is visible above and to the left. Although you are not above timberline, most of the rest of the hike is on open, treeless slopes. Try to get an early start to avoid afternoon thunderstorms in summer. If thunderstorms form, quickly retreat back down into the trees.

Several parallel trails climb steeply straight up the slope to the ridgetop. Follow them up to the ridge. The half-mile climb is probably the hardest part of the hike. The views to the south and west get better with every step. At the crest of the ridge, the trail improves and moderates its grade somewhat. It turns left and climbs north toward the summit on the back side of the ridge. At about 2.25 miles the trail crosses a ridge saddle back to the southwest-facing slope. A couple of long switchbacks bring you to the final approach. The trail passes through a fence gate a little before the top, and reaches the summit at about three miles.

Enjoy the incredible views. Mount Taylor is the highest peak for many miles in every direction. Unlike the bare grassy southwest slopes, the north and east slopes of the peak are densely forested with spruce, fir, and aspen. A grove of trees on the northwest side of the summit offers camping possibilities. A mile-long trail goes down the north ridge of Mount Taylor to the La Mosca

Lookout road. A forest of radio towers decorates the summit of nearby La Mosca Peak. Even though Mount Taylor is close and accessible to Albuquerque and I-40, it's surprising how few people use this trail. The bare grassy slopes of the peak would probably make excellent cross country ski routes in winter. Remember to keep an eye on the weather. Lightning and hail sent me scurrying for cover on my climb.

HIKE 30 *ZUNI-ACOMA TRAIL*

General description: A moderately difficult hike across the main lava flows at El Malpais National Monument.
General location: About sixteen miles south of Grants.
Length: About fourteen miles round trip.
Elevation: 6,920-6,880 feet..
Maps: National Park Service trail brochure, Arrosa Ranch and Los Pilares 7.5-minute USGS quads.
Best season: All year.
Water availability: None.
Special attractions: Rugged lava features; the trail is part of an ancient Indian trail; solitude.
Finding the trailhead: From the intersection of Interstate 40 and NM 53 on the west side of Grants, drive about sixteen miles south on NM 53. The marking parking area for the trail is on the left (east) side of the highway. To follow the hike in reverse, from the east trailhead, drive east of Grants about five miles on Interstate 40. At the NM 117 junction, go south on NM 117 about fifteen miles to the east trailhead. On the east side there isn't a parking lot, but a sign and ladder over the fence mark the trail.

The hike: The trail is part of the old Indian trail that connects the villages of Zuni and Acoma. It crosses five different lava flows, the most recent being only 700-1,000 years old. Since some of the pottery found along the trail is almost as old as the newest lava, the trail may be almost 1,000 years old.

Be sure to wear sturdy boots, since most of the trail surface consists of rough lava. Since the trail is often on rock, it can be relatively faint. Rock cairns, some hundreds of years old, and wooden posts mark the route. Travelling from west to east, the trail loses a small amount of elevation, but has a considerable number of small ups and downs as it crosses the lava flows.

The first lava flow at the start of the trail is the oldest in the valley. Although you walk on it for only a short time, it underlies many of the other flows that the trail crosses. Gnarled ponderosa pines, pinon pines, and junipers dot the lava for much of the hike.

The second lava flow, that issued from Twin Craters to the northwest, is younger and and less vegetated. Rough and chunky aa lava make up this flow. At about 2.5 miles the trail crosses onto the even younger Bandera Flow. This flow, coming from Bandera Crater to the northwest, contains extensive sytems of lava tubes.

The fourth and youngest flow, the McCarty Flow, is only about 700-1000 years old. This lava, called pahoehoe, has a ropey, frozen molasses-like texture

The Sandstone Bluffs overlook the lava flow crossed by the Zuni-Acoma Trail.

and is reached at about 3.5 miles. It flowed north from a vent about eight miles southwest. Finally, just before reaching the trail's end at NM 117, you cross onto the older Laguna Flow. It erupted from the Hoya de Cibola Volcano about fourteen miles west.

The trail ends at NM 117 at the base of the sandstone cliffs marking the east side of the broad lava-filled valley. By using a car shuttle, the trail distance can be halved to seven miles. Generally the trail can be hiked year-round. Occasional winter snows will make crossing difficult for a few days until it melts. The area can be very cold in winter, but also quite hot in summer, so prepare accordingly. The slight elevation change and moderate distance (especially when hiked one-way with a car shuttle) make the hike appear easy, but the rough lava and many small ups and downs are tiring.

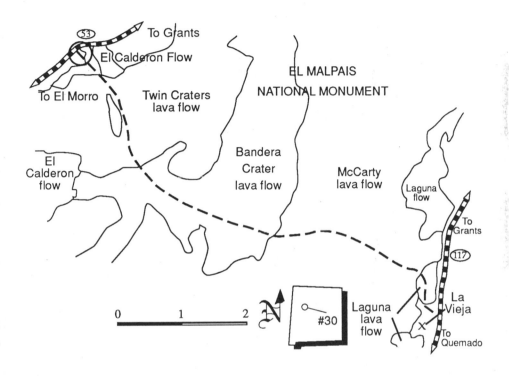

HIKE 31 *BIG SKYLIGHT CAVE*

General description: An easy day hike to an extensive lava tube cave system.
General location: About thirty-five miles southwest of Grants.
Length: One mile round trip to tube.
Elevation: 7,580-7,600 feet.
Maps: National Park Service "Big Tubes Area" brochure, Ice Caves 7.5-minute USGS quad.
Best season: All year when roads are dry.
Water availability: None.
Special attractions: Large lava tube caves.
Finding the trailhead: From Grants, take State Highway 53 south from Interstate 40 about twenty-seven miles to County Road 42. Follow the dirt county road about 6.5 miles to a small dirt road heading east through a gate. A high clearance vehicle is mandatory for the next 3.8 miles to the parking area. Be sure that your tires are in good condition. The lava rocks are jagged. Do not attempt after a heavy rain or snow; even a four wheel drive would have difficulty. Leave all gates as you find them. Several roads fork off to the right; bear left at the junctions. The parking area is marked with a "Big Lava Tubes" sign.

The hike: From the National Park Service "Big Lava Tubes" sign at the parking area, look for rock cairns heading east. Follow the cairns out onto the black lava flow. Watch carefully, so that you do not lose the cairns. You are entering a rolling sea of lava that is fairly heavily wooded with ponderosa pine, alligator juniper, and pinyon pine. It is easy to get lost if you lose the route. The trail is not worn into the lava flow; only the cairns mark the way. Be sure to take a compass and a topo map.

The marked route reaches the lava tube in about one-half mile. Just before you get to the tube, the cairns seem to go in two directions. Don't worry; they just go to different sections of the continuous tube.

The huge area of volcanoes and lava flows in El Malpais National Monument was formed over the past three million years in a series of many eruptions. The lava flows are new enough to be rough and jagged to hike over, but the area has been calm long enough for much of the area to become wooded with trees and shrubs. Lava tubes formed when the crust on the surface of the flow hardened, but the still-molten lava flowed out from underneath.

Big Skylight and Four Windows Caves, at the end of the trail, are just two openings into a lava tube over seventeen miles long, including collapsed sections. By following the tube, many other entrances can be found. Some of the entrances, such as Big Skylight, are deep pits requiring ropes to enter. However, you can find easy places to scramble down into the tubes at many of the entrances. The floors of the tubes are commonly boulder piles of loose shifting rock. Use extreme caution. To go beyond daylight in the tubes, be sure that each member of your party has a hard hat and three sources of light. A Coleman lantern has to be handled carefully while scrambling along the uneven floor, but will greatly help in lighting up the tubes. The dark colored rock and ceilings as high as forty feet easily soak up other smaller sources

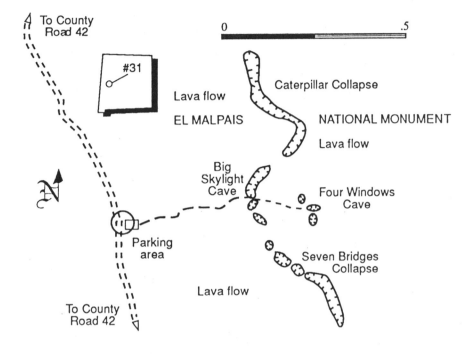

of light. If you exit the tube from an entrance different from the one you entered, be careful not to become lost on the surface.

HIKE 32 *LA LUZ TRAIL*

General description: A strenuous day hike or overnight trip through the Sandia Wilderness to the crest of the Sandia Mountains.

General location: The northeast side of Albuquerque.

Length: About fifteen miles round trip.

Elevation: 7,060-10,678 feet.

Maps: Sandia Mountain Wilderness, Cibola National Forest: Sandia-Mountainair District, Sandia Crest 7.5-minute USGS quad.

Best season: April through November.

Water availability: See text.

Special attractions: Views, passage through several life zones.

Finding the trailhead: From Interstate 40 on the east side of Albuquerque, take the Tramway Boulevard exit and follow it north 9.8 miles to paved FR 333. Follow FR 333 for 2.5 miles to the La Luz trailhead at the upper end of the Juan Tabo Picnic Ground. Lead-in signs direct you through the picnic area. Tramway Boulevard can also be reached from Interstate 25 and much of the rest of the city.

The hike: Even though a half-million people sprawl across the Rio Grande Valley at the base of the Sandias, much of the rugged west face of the mountains has remained wild. In 1978, Congress protected much of the area as the Sandia Mountain Wilderness, now 37,232 acres.

Tremendous faulting tilted the mountains high above the Rio Grande Valley. The steep and rugged west side exposes the bare bones of the earth's crust with enormous cliffs and pinnacles, while the east side slopes much more gently, with a softening coat of forest. Precambrian granite makes up most of the west face through which the trail climbs. A layer of Pennsylvanian limestone caps the crest.

Because of the large elevation gain on the trail, you'll pass through several of the west's major life zones as you go. The increased moisture and lower temperatures found at higher elevations creates different habitats. The trail starts in the Upper Sonoran Zone, characterized by semi-arid grasslands and scrubby forests of pinyon and juniper. Ponderosa pine typifies the Transition Zone, the next one up, although pinyon grows in the lower levels and Douglas fir grows in the upper levels. As the trail approaches the crest it moves into the Canadian Life Zone. Common trees here are Douglas fir, aspen, and blue spruce. Finally, on the crest, lies the Hudsonian Zone, with Engelmann spruce, sub-alpine fir, and other hardy trees.

Because of the proximity to Albuquerque, the trail is probably one of the most popular in the state, even though it is strenuous. Footraces are even held on the trail. Summer weekends are the busiest, naturally. The continuously changing views still make the trail a rewarding hike. Just relax and enjoy the cameraderie of other hikers. Some of the other trails in this book are so unused, you'll probably be happy to see people for a change.

In summer, try to get an early start, since the bottom half of the trail can be very hot and exposed. Also take some warm clothes and raingear because of the frequent summer thunderstorms on the crest.

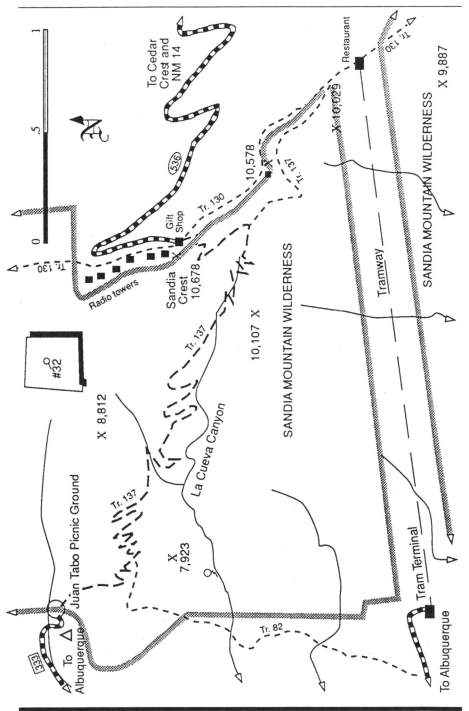

The upper tramway terminal at the end of the La Luz Trail makes a loop trip possible.

Looking up at the mountain from the parking lot, you'll wonder how the trail ever gets through the towering cliffs above. From the trailhead, the La Luz Trail, 137, immediately begins to climb at a moderate grade and never lets up. Another trail, the Piedra Lisa Trail also starts from the same trailhead. A little less than one mile up, Tramway Trail 82 turns off to the right. Stay with the La Luz Trail to Sandia Crest. Switchbacks start in earnest after the junction. Please don't shortcut the switchbacks, as it erodes the hillside.

At close to three miles up, the trail crosses a canyon that usually has some running water. Check with the Forest Service ahead of time before depending on it. In a pinch, water can be obtained at the gift shop on Sandia Crest. However, since they have to truck their water up the mountain, don't expect to get large quantities. Buying a soft drink or other item would be a nice gesture if you must ask for water.

No official junctions are encountered for the next six miles. However, here and there trails lead off the main route, usually to rock climbing destinations. The main trail is well-maintained and heavily used, so you shouldn't have any trouble staying with it. The trail slowly goes higher, finally climbing up a steep canyon through towering cliffs of reddish granite. Cooler temperatures and more trees make the second half of the climb more pleasant. If you're lucky, you may see a bighorn climbing on the crags above the trail.

Finally, at about seven miles, you'll reach the junction with Trail 84, the Crest Spur Trail. Turn left on it toward Sandia Crest. After struggling up the steep half-mile of Trail 84, you reach the summit, with its gift shop, radio towers, and crowds. If desired, a car shuttle can be arranged ahead of time to get back down, by driving up the back side of the mountains on NM 536. Alternately, rather than turning left onto the Crest Spur Trail, stay on the La Luz Trail for an additional one mile to the top of the tramway. Ride the tramway back down and hike the two miles back to your car on Trail 82, the Tramway Trail, mentioned at the start of the trail description.

HIKE 33 10-K TRAIL

General description: An easy loop hike into the northern section of the Sandia Mountain Wilderness.
General location: About thirty miles northwest of Albuquerque.
Length: About 6.5 miles round trip.
Elevation: 9,600-10,678 feet.
Maps: Sandia Mountain Wilderness, Cibola National Forest: Sandia-Mountainair District, Sandia Crest 7.5-minute USGS quad.
Best season: May through October.
Water availability: Media Spring.
Special attractions: Views, lush forest, excellent marked winter cross-country ski route.
Finding the trailhead: Go east out of the center of Albuquerque on Interstate 40 about fifteen miles to the turnoff to Cedar Crest on NM 14. Go left on NM 14 about six miles to the turnoff to Sandia Crest on NM 536. Follow paved NM 536 11.6 miles to the trailhead about two miles short of the crest. The 10-K Trail is marked by signs on both sides of the road in a huge swath cleared through the forest. Park in the rough parking lot in the cleared area on the right, or north, side of the highway.

The hike: The 10-K Trail got its name because it roughly follows the 10,000-foot elevation contour along the east side of the Sandias. The huge cleared strip was the initial work of a large scenic highway that was planned to run along much of the Sandia Crest. Fortunately the plan was killed before it was completed, even though the builders had already cleared an ugly strip several miles long through the forest.

The first part of the hike passes through dense forests of aspen, spruce, and Douglas fir. Most of the return loop follows the crest, with spectacular views of the Rio Grande Valley and beyond. From the parking area, look for the trail leading up into the woods from the uphill side of the cleared area right next to the highway. Don't follow the rough dirt road that heads down the cleared strip.

Once you get on the well-maintained trail, it's easy to follow. Blue plastic diamonds nailed to the trees mark the route for skiers in winter. At about 0.5 miles, the trail splits. Take either route; the forks quickly rejoin. Overall, the trail descends slightly for its first two miles. At almost two miles, a sign

A windswept Douglas fir tops the crest of the Sandia Mountains.

marks the Sandia Mountain Wilderness boundary. Just beyond, the trail forks. A short hike down to the right lies Media Spring. Check with the Forest Service ahead of time to find out its status.

Go left at the junction on the 10-K Trail and begin the short, but moderately steep climb to the crest. Less than 0.25 mile up, the trail crosses the ugly cleared strip. A few hundred yards up from the strip, a cross-country ski trail cuts in sharply from the left. Stay right on the 10-K trail. The 10-K Trail soon ends at about 2.5 miles at Crest Trail 130. Enjoy the incredible views from the rugged crest. The Jemez Mountains loom far to the north, while Mt. Taylor is usually visible far to the west.

Go left on the Crest Trail toward Sandia Crest, climbing some as you go. The trail breaks in and out of the forest, mixing great views with lush forest. The trail passes a virtual forest of radio towers on the right for the last 0.5 mile to Sandia Crest. The Crest, at the end of the highway, is the highest point on the hike and in the Sandias. A gift shop and crowds decorate the summit. Return to the trailhead by walking 2.2 miles back down NM 536 to your car. Experienced hikers, armed with the topo map or wilderness map, can cut across the highway switchbacks and shorten the return by bushwhacking through the forest. An similar, alternate loop can be done by following the 10-K Trail south to the crest and returning by the Crest Trail.

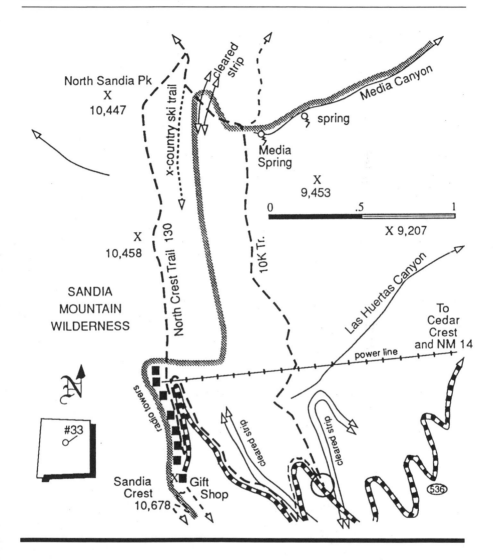

North Sandia Pk
X
10,447

x-country ski trail

cleared strip

Media Canyon

spring

Media Spring

X
9,453

0   .5   1

X 9,207

North Crest Trail 130

X
10,458

SANDIA
MOUNTAIN
WILDERNESS

10K Tr.

Las Huertas Canyon

To
Cedar
Crest
and NM 14

power line

N

#33

radio towers

cleared strip

cleared strip

536

Sandia
Crest
10,678

X Gift
Shop

HIKE 34 TREE SPRING TRAIL

General description: A moderate day hike to the top of the Sandia Peak Tramway.

General location: About twenty-five miles east of Albuquerque.

Length: About six miles round trip.

Elevation: 8,460-10,290 feet.

Maps: Cibola National Forest: Sandia-Mountainair Ranger Districts, Sandia Mountain Wilderness, Sandia Crest 7.5-minute USGS quad.

Best season: May to November.

Water availability: Restaurant and visitor center at top of tramway, when open.

Special attractions: Views, lush forest.

Finding the trailhead: Go west about fifteen miles from the center of Albuquerque on I-40 to the NM 14/Cedar Crest exit. Exit and turn left, or north, on NM 14. Go about 5.9 miles on NM 14 to the NM 536 fork on the left. Follow NM 536 toward Sandia Crest. At about 5.7 miles, park at the well-marked Tree Spring Trail 147 trailhead on the left.

The hike: Most of the trails to the crest in the Sandia Mountains are fairly long and strenuous. The Tree Spring Trail is the easiest route to the crest (other than driving up NM 536 or taking the tramway). It reaches the crest a little more than halfway up this hike after gaining only about 1,000 feet. The trail is well-maintained and follows a steady moderate grade to the crest. Because of its proximity to Albuquerque, however, don't expect to have it to yourself.

The trailhead has a paved parking area and even a bathroom. Be sure that your valuables are out of sight; a temporary sign says 'Experiencing break-ins—protect your valuables.'

The trailhead signs are slightly off in their mileages. The trail starts climbing through lush Douglas fir, and reaches the marked Oso Corridor Trail forking off to the left about 0.3 mile up. The trail does not appear on maps. Stay right, toward the Crest Trail.

At a little less than two miles, you hit the marked Sandia Mountain Wilderness boundary at a four-way intersection. To the left, Crest Trail 130 goes thirteen miles all the way to Canyon Estates. It makes a great backpack with a car shuttle or ride at the end. Straight ahead, Trail 130 goes up to the tramway about one mile away (the sign distance of 0.5 mile is wrong). This will be your return route. Turn right on the 10K Trail. The 10K Trail is marked with blue plastic diamonds for cross-country ski use in winter.

Go a little less than 0.75 mile along the relatively level 10K Trail to an unmarked fork. Take either fork; they quickly rejoin when they hit the downhill ski trails of the Sandia ski area. Turn left at the ski runs and follow the runs up the mountain to the crest at the top of the ski area. The half mile climb up the grassy ski run is steep and the air is getting thin, so take your time.

At the top, views open up in all directions. A visitor center crowns the crest at the top terminal of the tramway that comes up from Albuquerque, below to the west. The Cibola National Forest visitor center has interesting exhibits about the Sandia Mountains. Since the summit isn't exactly a wilderness

HIKE 34 *TREE SPRING TRAIL*

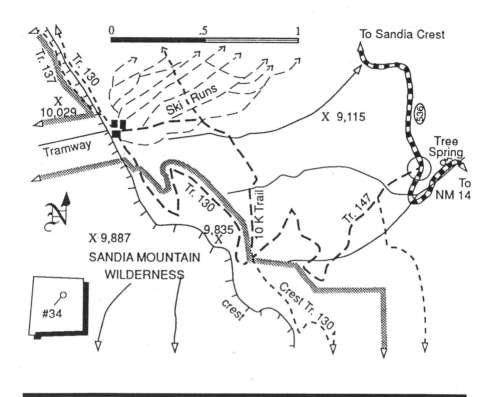

anyway, why not join the crowd and enjoy lunch at the High Finance Restaurant before hiking back down.

To return, follow Trail 130 down the crest to the south, away from the summit buildings. In about 0.25 mile you re-enter the wilderness. The trail descends at a moderate grade through dense forest to the same four-way junction described earlier. Go straight ahead, back down Tree Spring Trail 147. If you wish to avoid the steep climb up the ski run on your way up, just follow Trail 130 to the tramway, rather than the 10K Trail and the ski run.

HIKE 35 *MANZANO PEAK*

General description: A moderate day hike to the highest point in the Manzano Mountains.

General location: About sixty-five miles southeast of Albuquerque.

Length: About 7.25 miles round trip.

Elevation: 8,080-10,098 feet.

Maps: Manzano Mountain Wilderness, Cibola National Forest: Sandia-Mountainair District, Manzano Peak 7.5-minute USGS quad.

Best season: April through November.

Water availability: Unreliable-see text.

Special attractions: Views, lush forest, solitude.

Finding the trailhead: Drive about twelve miles north of Mountainair on NM 55 to Manzano. Turn left on gravel FR 253 and drive five miles to the marked FR 422 turnoff. Go left on gravel FR 422 for 3.8 miles to its junction with FR 275 and park.

The hike: The forty-mile long Manzano Mountains are an extension of the fault block that raised the Sandia Mountains to the north. The mountains appear deceptively small and uninteresting from a distance. However, the mountains' long crest maintains an altitude of 9,000-10,000 feet. Lush forest covers the slopes and several canyons have small streams. The 36,970-acre Manzano Mountain Wilderness protects the heart of the range.

The word manzano means "apple" in Spanish. In the 1700s, explorers found very old apple trees growing in a village on the eastern side of the mountains. Since apples are not native to North America, the visitors were unable to determine how the apple trees appeared. Most probably, the apples were brought in by early Spanish explorers and settlers.

The area surrounding the Manzano Mountains was one of the first places settled in the United States. Spaniards established missions at Quarai, Abo, and other sites at the foot of the mountains in the early 1600s. If you have time, be sure to visit the ruins, protected in Salinas Pueblo Missions National Monument.

From the FR 422 and FR 275 junction, turn right (west) and walk up the rough extension of FR 275. The trail begins in heavily logged new-growth ponderosa. High clearance vehicles can usually make it up to the road's end about 0.6 mile toward the mountains. About 0.5 mile up, marked Trail 73 forks off to the left. Continue a short distance up the road to its end in a little clearing.

Trail 80, the Kayser Mill Trail, climbs up out of the left side of the clearing back toward the valley. A sign marks its start. The trail quickly turns back toward the mountains and begins climbing. The excellent trail climbs steadily for the entire 2.25 miles to the crest. About 0.5 mile beyond the end of the road, a sign marks the wilderness boundary.

The trail travels through lush forests of Douglas fir, aspen, and spruce for most of the climb. Right before the trail crosses a large rockslide near the crest, it contours around the head of a small drainage in a clearing. An unreliable spring is visible just below the trail in the creek bottom. Check with the Forest Service about its status before you start. When it's flowing, it helps overnight campers immensely because it's close to the crest.

The trail reaches the crest in a large meadow on a saddle at almost three miles. Go straight up the 9,800-foot elevation meadow to signs marking the Crest Trail, 170. The saddle and rest of the crest make excellent camping areas. Most of the rest of the hike is not level enough. Be careful about lightning on the crest. The views from the saddle are impressive, but the vista from Manzano Peak easily tops them.

From the saddle, go left (south) and follow the crest trail to the summit of Manzano Peak. A little more than 0.5 mile along the crest, Trail 170A forks downward to the right. Stay left for the last 0.25 mile to the summit.

HIKE 35 *MANZANO PEAK*

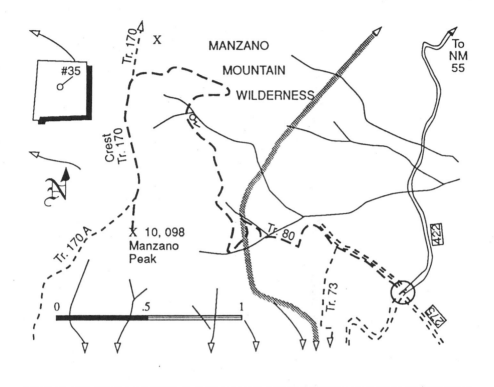

After the long hike through the densely wooded mountains, the bare, rocky peak is a pleasant surprise. With few trees, the views are unbeatable. The mountains fall away abruptly to the east, south, and west. On clear days, mountains as far away as Sierra Blanca, the San Mateos, Mt. Taylor, and the Sangre de Cristos rise prominently on the horizon. Oddly enough, tiny cacti cover the bare summit. A mail box that someone placed on the summit adds a comic touch. Don't worry about crowds. The register inside the box indicates light visitation. I climbed the peak in mid-June and the most recent signature I found was made two weeks earlier.

An alternate, but considerably longer route turns the hike into a loop trip if desired. Take Trail 170A down off the peak to FR 422. Go left up FR 422 about 0.5 mile to Trail 73 on the left. Follow Trail 73 to FR 275 and the trailhead. The alternate route is about four miles longer and involves some climbing on Trail 73.

HIKE 36 *RED CANYON*

General description: A moderate day hike through heavy forest to the wilderness crest of the Manzano Mountains.

General location: About 60 miles southeast of Albuquerque.

Length: About 7.5 miles round trip.

Elevation: 8,000-9960 feet.

Maps: Manzano Mountain Wilderness, Cibola National Forest: Sandia-Mountainair District, Capilla Peak and Manzano Peak 7.5 minute USGS quads.

Best season: April through November.

Water availability: Spruce Spring, Red Canyon.

Special attractions: Views, lush forest, small waterfalls.

Finding the trailhead: Drive north of Mountainair about twelve miles on NM 55 to Manzano. Turn left on gravel FR 253 and drive 5.9 miles to the Red Canyon Campground. Signs mark the way.

Cornhusk lilies grow at Spruce Spring in the Manzano Mountain Wilderness.

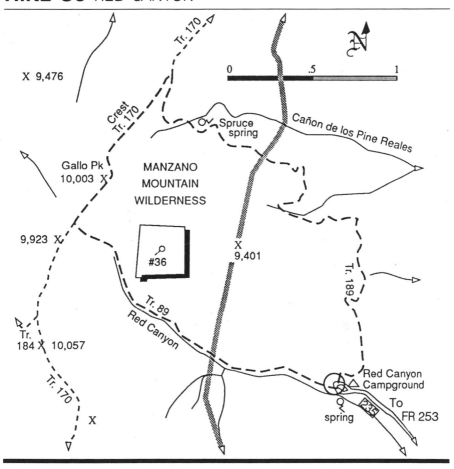

The hike: The Manzano Mountains are an unassuming range with hidden surprises. This hike provides great views, lush forest, and even two small waterfalls. The campground at the trailhead lies in dense forest and is a pleasant place to camp either before or after your hike. At the time of my visit in the summer of 1990, potable water was not available.

However, a good spring by the creek in the campground could be used, along with purification. The trail starts at the upper end of the campground loop.

Follow the signs for Spruce Trail 189 up out of the campground. The trail winds its way to the crest at a very mild grade through ponderosa, aspen, Douglas fir, and spruce. About three miles up the trail, a sign marks Spruce Spring on the right. A 300-foot side trail leads down to the spring. The trail reaches the crest soon after, at almost 3.5 miles, and intersects with Crest Trail 170. The crest is open and grassy at the junction, providing great views to the east and west. Level areas along the crest near the junction provide the best campsites on this hike.

Turn left (south) on the Crest Trail and follow it as it climbs up toward Gallo Peak. The crest is exposed to lightning, so be aware of developing thunderstorms. At close to a mile up Trail 170, the route hits its high point when it crests an east-trending ridge. A short scramble up the ridge to the right will take you to the summit of 10,003-foot Gallo Peak. A short descent from the ridge brings Trail 170 to another grassy saddle with views to the east and west. The saddle area, at almost five miles, provides the other good camping area along the hike.

From the grassy saddle, turn left onto Trail 89 to return to the Red Canyon Campground. Trail 89 drops more steeply than the Spruce Trail and is more heavily used. About one mile down, the trail reaches the bottom of Red Canyon. The trail follows the canyon the rest of the way, accompanied by a small running stream in all but the driest years. The canyon becomes lush, wet, narrow, and rocky. Two small waterfalls drop off ledges along the way. The trail ends at the campground at about 7.5 miles.

HIKE 37 *FOURTH OF JULY*

General description: A moderate day hike to the crest of the Manzano Mountains through some of the best fall color in the Southwest.
General location: About 55 miles southeast of Albuquerque.
Length: About 6.25 miles round trip.
Elevation: 7,520-8,660 feet.
Maps: Manzano Mountain Wilderness, Cibola National Forest: Sandia-Mountainair District, Bosque Peak 7.5-minute USGS quad.
Best season: April through November.
Water availability: Upper Fourth of July Spring, Big Spring.
Special attractions: Bigtooth maples, views, lush forest.
Finding the trailhead: Follow the same directions as for Hike 38, except drive 0.5 mile further up FR 55 to Fourth of July Campground. Drive 0.4 mile to the upper end of the campground and park.

The hike: The Manzano Mountains area around the upper ends of Tajique and Torreon Canyons boasts one of the best stands of bigtooth maples in the Southwest. The trees turn rich shades of scarlet and gold in the fall. The campground itself is well-wooded with maples. Because of the fall color, the trails around the campground are very popular on fall weekends. The excellent trail traverses miles of beautiful forest, making it a worthwhile hike any time of year. On a summer weekday, only one other vehicle shared the campground with me and I only saw one couple on the trail.

The marked trailhead for Trail 173 is at the upper end of the campground. The trail follows the canyon bottom up into the mountains. A stream usually flows part way down, fed by Upper Fourth of July Spring. You soon pass the spring, obvious with its small tank used by livestock. Just past it is the Manzano Mountain Wilderness boundary. A new trail that connects with the Albuquerque Trail comes in from the right (See Hike 38). Continue up the canyon on Trail 173 to the junction with Trail 79 at almost 1.5 miles. Turn right and follow the signs uphill toward the Crest Trail.

The Manzano Range is larger and lusher than it appears from a distance.

Maples almost solidly forest the next half mile. At about two miles, turn right onto Crest Trail 170 at the intersection. The mileages on the different signs don't quite agree with each other. The trail levels out for the next 0.25 miles to a saddle in the crest. Enjoy the tremendous views of the Rio Grande and Estancia Valleys. Just above the saddle to the north rises a subsummit of Mosca Peak. Farther away, to the north-northwest, rises Guadalupe Peak. Be careful not to get confused at the saddle. Several trails wind through the oak scrub.

Retrace your route back to Trail 79. Follow 79 all the way down the mountain, instead of turning off on Trail 173. The descent down Trail 79 is relatively mild, except for a short steep stretch about halfway down where it drops into a canyon. Maples forest much of the canyon bottom. A small stream usually comes and goes. An unmarked trail joins the main trail on the right just before reaching FR 55. At about 4.25 miles you reach FR 55. Big Spring lies right across the road from Trail 79. Go left on FR 55 about 1.4 miles to the Fourth of July Campground entrance. The road is a pleasant downhill walk along a permanent stream lined with maples.

The loop can be enlarged considerably by continuing south on the Crest Trail 170 to Trail 174. Go left and down on Trail 174 to FR 55. Follow FR 55 left back to the campground. Alternately, Trails 79, 170, and 174 make a good loop day hike, when combined with a short stretch of FR 55.

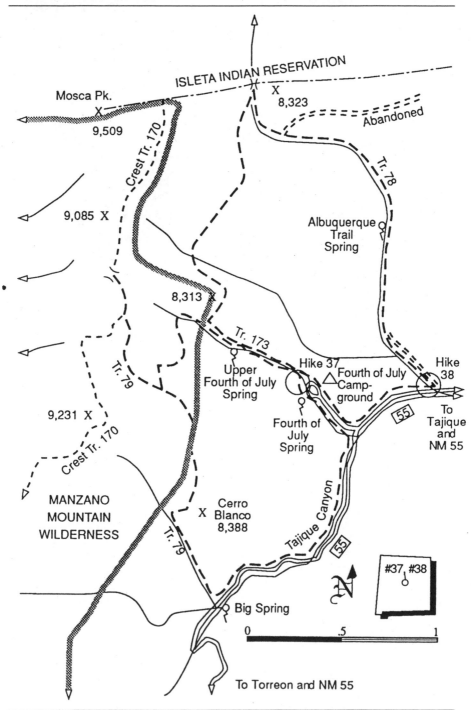

Mosca Pk.
X
9,509

Crest Tr. 170

ISLETA INDIAN RESERVATION

X
8,323

Abandoned

Tr. 78

9,085 X

Albuquerque
Trail
Spring

8,313

Tr. 173

Tr. 79

Upper
Fourth of July
Spring

Hike 37

Fourth of July
Camp-
ground

Hike
38

To Tajique
and
NM 55

Fourth of
July
Spring

55

9,231 X

Crest Tr. 170

MANZANO
MOUNTAIN
WILDERNESS

Cerro
X Blanco
8,388

Tajique Canyon

55

Tr. 79

N

#37 #38

Big Spring

0   .5   1

To Torreon and NM 55

HIKE 38 ALBUQUERQUE TRAIL

General description: An easy day hike into an area of bigtooth maples noted for their fall color.
General location: About fifty-five miles southeast of Albuquerque.
Length: About 5.25 miles round trip.
Elevation: 7,420-8,250 feet.
Maps: Manzano Mountain Wilderness, Cibola National Forest: Sandia-Mountainair District, Tajique and Bosque Peak 7.5-minute USGS quads.
Best season: April through November.
Water availability: Albuquerque Trail Spring, Upper Fourth of July Spring.
Special attractions: Bigtooth maples.
Finding the trailhead: Go east on Interstate 40 about fifteen miles from the center of Albuquerque to NM 337. Turn right and follow it about thirty miles to NM 55. Turn right and follow NM 55 about three miles into Tajique. Turn right on gravel FR 55, marked with a Fourth of July Campground sign, and follow it west into the mountains. At 6.9 miles, park along the road at the Albuquerque Trail 78 sign (just short of the campground entrance).

The hike: The northern end of the Manzano Mountains is noted for its impressive stands of bigtooth maples. The maples provide some of the best fall color in the southwest. This loop trail climbs at an easy grade up through conifer forest to some dense stands of the trees.

The first 0.4 mile of the trail follows a rough dirt road. Unless it's wet, a high clearance vehicle can make it.

At 0.4 mile, the Forest Service has gated the old logging road and converted the road to a trail with recent construction work. A very small stream usually flows down the creek bottom. The old road used to follow much of the bottom and was wet and muddy in places. The Forest Service has raised the new trail slightly out of the bottom. Initially, the forest you pass through has signs of fairly recent logging, but the trail eventually leaves it behind. The most common conifers are ponderosa and Douglas fir.

A short distance up the trail, you pass the spring that creates the stream, Albuquerque Trail Spring. On this short a hike, I recommend that you carry water, rather than bother to purify the spring water. After you get about a mile up the trail, maples begin to appear. At a little more than 1.5 miles, a faint abandoned road comes in from the right. Stay left, following the signs marking Trail 78 up the canyon bottom. The next half mile is particularly nice, with dense stands of maples. Often they even arch over the trail. Try to come on fall weekdays, because the area is popular on the weekends.

The trail appears to end at a fence at about two miles. The fence marks the boundary of the Isleta Indian Reservation. Don't cross it without permission. The Forest Service has just completed an extension of Trail 78 from the end of the trail. It's not shown on any of the current maps. From the fence, the new trail cuts left up the hillside. It traverses the mountain slopes to Trail 173 above Fourth of July Campground at about 3.5 miles. The trail intersects Trail 173 at the wilderness boundary just above Upper Fourth of July Spring. Turn left and follow Trail 173 downhill into the campground at about 4.25 miles, walk down through the campground to FR 55, and go left on the road about 0.5 mile to your car at the trailhead. Trail 173 is the start of another hike in this book, 37.

On quiet days, keep an eye out for bears in the Manzano Mountains. I surprised a young bear (and myself!) on this trail one summer afternoon.

Black bears, such as this one in the Manzano Mountains, make frequent campground raids in New Mexico mountains. Keep your food out of reach.

HIKE 39 *NORTH BALDY*

General description: A moderate day hike along the crest of the Magdalena Mountains.

General location: About thirty miles west of Socorro.

Length: About eleven miles round trip.

Elevation: 10,420-9320 feet.

Maps: Cibola National Forest-Magdalena Ranger District, Magdalena and South Baldy 7.5-minute USGS quads.

Best season: May to November.

Water availability: None.

Special attractions: Solitude, views, lush forest.

Finding the trailhead: From Socorro, take US 60 15.6 miles west toward Magdalena to the Water Canyon turnoff (unmarked during my last visit in September, 1990). Turn left and follow the paved road, FR 235, for 12.6 miles to the marked North Baldy trailhead. The pavement ends at 4.8 miles at the attractive Water Canyon Campground. The remaining 7.8 miles of improved dirt road is usually passable by any vehicle during the warm months. Check with the Forest Service office in Magdalena first. Drive the narrow, windy road slowly and carefully, watching for rocks. The first couple of miles past the campground were the worst during my September visit.

The hike: The North Baldy Trail was the last hike that I did for this guidebook. If I had known how beautiful the Magdalena Mountains were beforehand, I would have left room for another hike or two.

The Magdalena Mountains are a fairly small range in area, but with a top elevation of 10,783 feet are the third highest range in southern New Mexico. The mountains rise abruptly from the surrounding grassy plains. Numerous old mines, most long abandoned, lie scattered throughout the mountains. The old ghost town of Kelly, on the north side of the range, boomed and died intermittently until the last few mines closed in the 1950s.

FR 235 goes only a short distance beyond the trailhead before being blocked by a gate. Just beyond the gate lies the astronomical and atmospheric research facilities of the Langmuir Research Site. Langmuir Laboratory, operated by New Mexico Tech, specializes in lightning and thunderstorm studies.

The trail starts at the sign on the right side of the road. It climbs steeply uphill to the left from the parking area. The trail is lightly used and tends to fade out in open grassy areas such as the slope above the trailhead. Follow the marker arrow on the sign just up the slope from the trailhead. Rock cairns help mark the way. Don't let the short steep thin-air climb above the trailhead discourage you; most of the rest of the trail is easier. At the crest of the ridge, still in view of your car, you hit the highest point of the hike. From the ridge, the now clearly visible trail drops down the other side into lush spruce and fir forest. The trail soon pops out onto a meadow on the long north-south crest of the range.

The rest of the trail follows the crest all the way to North Baldy. Beware of lightning on this exposed hike, especially on summer afternoons. Most of the trail consists of long level stretches with occasional downhills to the low point at the saddle below North Baldy. The little-used trail tends to fade out in the occasional open grassy saddles and hilltops. Just keep following the crest and sooner or later you'll find the trail again. Rock cairns and tree blazes will help.

When you first hit the crest, in an open meadow, the trail makes a switchback down the west slope before continuing north through the woods just below the crest. It's easy to miss the faint switchback; if you do, just follow the faint trail on the very top of the crest that was made by other people who missed the proper trail. At about a mile, the two routes rejoin in a large grassy saddle. A sign marks Trail 10 forking down off the crest to the right. Continue north through the grass along the crest, watching carefully for cairns until the trail reenters the forest. At about two miles, the trail hits a new-looking mine road that crosses over a saddle in the crest. The road doesn't show on any maps. Follow the road to the right (east) for 100 feet or so, just over the top of the crest. Look closely below the edge of the road on the left. The trail and a sign will be visible, about fifty feet below the crest on the east slope.

Scramble down the road embankment to the trail and continue north. At a little less that three miles, Trail 26 forks off left. Stay right, on the crest on Trail 8. Just a bit further along, Trail 25 also forks off to the left. Again, stay right, on the crest. At a little over four miles, the trail begins its descent to a saddle, the lowest point of the hike.

The last 0.75 mile of the hike climbs 500 feet from the saddle to the 9,858-foot summit of North Baldy and the old four-wheel-drive mine road that climbs up over the peak. Much of the last climb crosses a treeless slope. The view from the top, and much of the trail along the crest, is spectacular, with views from the Sandia Mountains to the San Mateos.

No water sources lie along the trail, but backpackers armed with topo maps should be able to find water in springs below the crest. Check with the Forest Service about their status. Come visit the empty Magdalena Mountains and give the overused Sandia Mountains and Pecos Wilderness a rest. The Magdalenas are only a two-hour drive from Albuquerque. Trails 11, 70, and 93 are also accessible from FR 235 and promise to be beautiful routes. A strenuous, but spectacular, loop backpack is possible using trails 11, 15, 12, and 14.

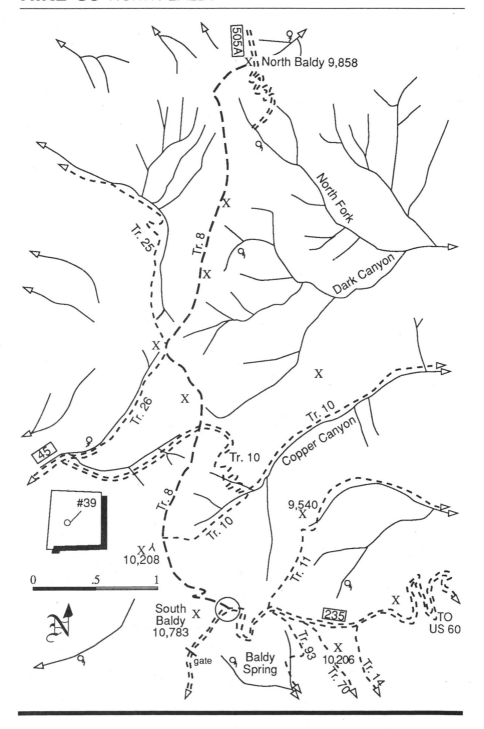

HIKE 40 *MOUNT WITHINGTON*

General description: A strenuous overnight hike through the obscure Withington Wilderness.

General location: About thirty-five miles southwest of Magdalena.

Length: About fourteen miles round trip.

Elevation: 6,720-10,119 feet.

Maps: Cibola National Forest—Magdalena Ranger District, Mount Withington 7.5-minute USGS quad.

Best season: Mid-April through November.

Water availability: See text.

Special attractions: Solitude, seasonal waterfall, views, forest.

Finding the trailhead: From Magdalena, drive 12.3 miles west on US 60 to the marked turnoff on the left to Mount Withington (FR 549). Follow FR 549 about 8.6 miles south to the marked FR 52 turnoff on the left. FR 549 is an excellent gravel road, although it may get a little muddy in spots with rain. Follow FR 52 for about 10.8 miles to the marked FR 56 turnoff on the right. Follow FR 56 down into Big Rosa Canyon for about 2.8 miles to the trailhead, marked with a Potato Canyon Trail 38 sign. FR 52 and FR 56 are usually in good condition and passable with any vehicle if care is used. Call the Forest Service in Magdalena for current conditions.

The hike: The San Mateo Range is one of the least visited in New Mexico. One beautiful September day, my mother and I spent several hours driving eighty miles of improved dirt roads in the north end of the mountains around Mount Withington and saw only one pickup. Two wilderness areas lie in the mountains, the Apache Kid in the south (see Hike 41) and the Withington in the north. Only two trails pass through the Withington Wilderness, the longer of which is described in this hike. The Withington Wilderness is very probably the least visited in the state.

Potato Canyon Trail 38 is very strenuous if hiked in its entirety as a round trip. However, the first four miles make an easy to moderate hike, since most of the climb is in the last three miles. A car shuttle can also be run to the top of the hike, halving the distance.

This trail is the place where you go to escape your in-laws and the IRS. The trail is so little-used that it's hard to follow in places. Except for the top around Mount Withington, you will probably never see anyone on this trail.

The second half of the hike should only be done if an expert hiker is with your party. The topographic map and a compass are necessities. Although the trail is a relatively straightforward hike up a canyon to the crest, it's easy to lose the trail.

The first 4.5 miles follow the canyon bottom, much of the way with no visible trail. Tree blazes mark the route fairly well, but you must look for them. From the trailhead, an old road leads about 0.3 mile up the canyon to the marked wilderness boundary. Continue upstream on the flat canyon floor, keeping an eye out for tree blazes. For the first three miles it's not especially important to stay with the marked route, since it just follows the canyon bottom. The blazes just serve as reassurance that you're on the proper route.

Walking in some canyon bottoms can be a nightmare, with either soft, mushy sand and gravel or ankle-turning cobbles and boulders. The alluvial sediment in Potato Canyon, however, is composed of flat, light-colored, shaly-looking rock and gravel that makes a smooth and firm walking surface. The gravel must occasionally wash down in tremendous floods because it has buried tree trunks several feet deep in places, creating an odd looking canyon floor. Some blazes were visible at ankle-height, instead of eye-level.

The canyon bottom starts in scattered pinyon-juniper and occasional ponderosas. As it climbs, the ponderosas and deciduous trees thicken, eventually grading into Douglas fir.

Overall, with a few exceptions, the canyon narrows as it climbs. At about 1.8 miles the canyon makes a major fork. Go left, following the blazes. Most other forks are minor; stay with the main canyon and the blazes. A spring with a trough is at about 2.25 miles in a narrow part of the canyon. The spring is seasonal, so check with the Forest Service ahead of time about its status. An old ruined cabin will be encountered on the right at almost three miles. When the canyon narrows into a small gorge, the trail bypasses it by climbing the left wall. It's actually easier just to stay in the canyon bottom. A small stream often flows in this stretch.

After surmounting a few boulders, you will encounter a small waterfall at about 3.25 miles, beautiful if it's flowing.

Scramble around the waterfall and continue up the little gorge. Be sure to get water here if you need it; it's the last chance. Remember, this stream is seasonal. The gorge quickly ends and the official trail drops back into the canyon bottom from the left wall. The trees in the canyon bottom are now much thicker. Many excellent campsites lie just above the gorge. Don't camp in the bottom; find a site up on the benches in case of floods. The buried trees serve as a warning.

The canyon forks again just above the gorge. Stay in the right fork, following the blazes. From here on, make an effort to follow the tree blazes. The trail frequently lies on the benches, slightly up out of the creek bottom. The canyon will start to get a little steeper and rockier, making travel on the benches easier. It crosses from bank to bank.

If you lose the blazes, backtrack and look carefully. The route is fairly well marked. At about 4.5 miles, the canyon leaves the stream bottom for good and begins switchbacking up to the crest. Watch carefully; you don't want to miss this point. The last 1.5 miles to the crest climbs through lush Douglas fir, with views to the east. The trail is faint, but generally visible. Some deadfalls will probably lie across the little-maintained route. The trail switchbacks up with a steep, but steady, grade all the way to the top. If you lose the trail, backtrack a bit. You probably missed a faint switchback.

The trail reaches the top and FR 138 in a forested saddle on the crest. A water cache could be hidden here ahead of time for multi-day backpackers. Signs mark the trailhead on FR 138, for those wishing to do the hike in reverse. Camping is possible on level areas along the crest. Views open up to the west. From here, follow the road to the right (north) toward Mount Withington. At about 0.6 mile, turn right onto FR 138B, and climb the last 0.2 mile to the lookout tower on the summit. If you want to avoid the road, just follow the crest uphill to the right from the saddle and you'll reach the peak. Tremendous views in every direction spread out below the grassy summit.

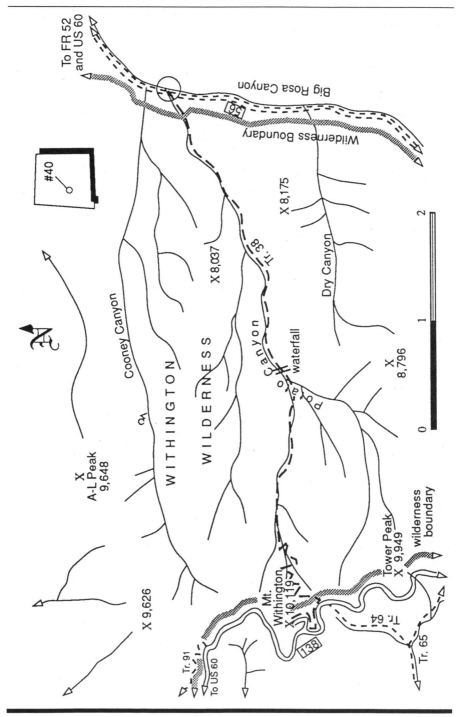

Come visit the Withington Wilderness. Give the heavily-used Sandia, Jemez, and Sangre de Cristo Mountains a rest. If at least a few people don't use these trails, the Forest Service will probably abandon them altogether. Don't worry about getting lost on the first half of the hike. Even if you lose the trail, provided that you never leave the canyon bottom, all you have to do find your car is follow the canyon downstream to the road. An excellent two or three day backpacking loop would take Trail 38 to FR 138 on the crest, travelling south (left) on FR 138 about two miles to Trail 37 on the left, descending Trail 37 down Water Canyon to FR 56, and following FR 56 down Big Rosa Canyon to the Trail 38 trailhead.

HIKE 41 SAN MATEO PEAK

General description: A strenuous day hike or overnight trip to a high peak in the heart of the Apache Kid Wilderness.
General location: About forty miles northwest of Truth or Consequences.
Length: About eight miles round trip.
Elevation: 7,360-10,139 feet.
Maps: Cibola National Forest—Magdalena Ranger District, Vicks Peak 7.5-minute USGS quad.
Best season: Mid-April through November.
Water availability: San Mateo Spring—see text.
Special attractions: Views, solitude, dense forest.
Finding the trailhead: From the north side of Truth or Consequences, take I-25 north a little more than twenty miles to Exit 100. Leave the freeway and get onto the old highway paralleling the interstate on the west side. Turn right, or north, on the old highway and follow it for about 4.8 miles to the FR 225 turnoff to Springtime Campground. Turn left on gravel FR 225 and follow it about 13.4 miles to the Springtime Campground entrance, FR 225A. Turn right onto the campground road and drive to the campground, about 0.5 mile.

For an alternate and very scenic route to take when you leave, drive south on the continuation of FR 225 to FR 139, Monticello, and ultimately I-25. The Cibola National Forest map shows the route. With care, improved FR 225 is usually quite good and passable with any vehicle. The southern approach, through Monticello, is usually rougher. Call about road status ahead of time.

From Socorro, follow I-25 south to Exit 115. Get onto the old highway paralleling the freeway and follow it south to FR 225, the Springtime Campground turnoff described above.

The hike: The forty-five-mile long San Mateo Mountains stretch from the high Plains of San Augustin to the Rio Grande Valley above Elephant Butte Lake. The mountains surrounding Mount Taylor (see Hike 29) have the same name, but are a completely different range. The mountains form a long chain of steep forested peaks. Vicks Peak, just south of San Mateo Peak, was named for the Apache chief Victorio, who used these mountains as hunting grounds and as a refuge. A few old mines, scattered around Vicks Peak and Rosedale Canyon, never produced much.

HIKE 41 *SAN MATEO PEAK*

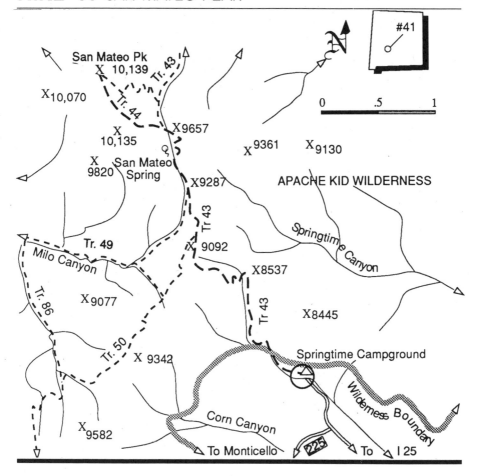

The heart of the south end of the range lies in the Apache Kid Wilderness, while part of the northern end lies in the Withington Wilderness (see Hike 40). The Apache Kid Wilderness contains 44,650 acres and is named after the Apache Kid, an Indian who was killed and buried near Blue Mountain. A little-used trail system of sixty-eight miles criss-crosses the wilderness.

The trail to San Mateo Peak, described here, is the most popular in the mountains, which doesn't mean much. The San Mateos are one of the least visited mountain ranges in New Mexico. What little visitation occurs is usually restricted to the roads and campgrounds. Even on summer weekends, you will probably see few people on this trail.

Other trails are even more likely to be deserted. Come to the San Mateos for solitude.

Well-marked Trail 43 starts at the sign in Springtime Campground. The campground is a small, beautiful, and quiet place with shelters, picnic tables, and pit toilets. The trail starts up the canyon above the campground through ponderosa pine. At about 0.25 mile you pass the marked wilderness boundary.

The stream flows part of the year. The trail is well-maintained and easy to follow. The trail quickly leaves the canyon bottom and begins a steep two-mile climb, gaining something like 1,700 feet. Finally, sweating and puffing, you will reach the crest at about 2.25 miles. If you can make it this far, you're home free. The crest is level enough for camping.

The grade levels out and the trail intersects with Trail 50 just over the crest. A chewed-up sign marks the fork.

Stay right, toward San Mateo Peak and Lookout. The next half mile to the junction with Trail 49 is easy. Stay right toward San Mateo Peak and begin climbing again at a moderate grade. Just past the junction, you pass the ruins of an old cabin and then you hit San Mateo Spring. The spring has a concrete and stone horse trough fed by a pipe. The spring dries up during dry spells and sometimes in early summer. Don't count on it without checking with the Forest Service in Magdalena first. Two other springs lie along Trail 50 to the south.

The trail switchbacks fairly steeply up from the spring to the well-marked junction with Trail 44 at about 3.25 miles.

Plenty of level campsites lie around the junction. The right hand fork to Blue Mountain is the continuation of Trail 43.

Turn left on more-heavily traveled Cowboy Trail 44 to the peak and lookout. The trail enters a dense stand of aspen and climbs the last 0.75 mile through lush forest at a moderate grade.

The large flat summit contains a lookout tower and Forest Service cabin. Please don't disturb the facilities. The sixty-foot tower is missing the lower part of its ladder and is dangerous to climb. The forest opens up on the north side of the summit, giving a good view of Blue Mountain. Camping is possible on the summit and about 0.25 mile back down the trail in a fairly level area of woods.

Since you have to make quite an effort to get up to the top, bring a backpack and plan to stay a few days. Trail 43 can be followed along the crest for miles to the north and Trail 50 can be followed south. A good two or three day loop involves following Trail 43 north to Trail 48. Follow Trail 48 down Indian Creek to FR 225 and walk back up FR 225 to Springtime Campground.

A fire lookout crowns San Mateo Peak in the Apache Kid Wilderness.

HIKE 42 *SIGNAL PEAK*

General description: A moderate day hike to the summit of one the highest peaks in the Pinos Altos Range.
General location: About fifteen miles north of Silver City.
Length: Five miles round trip.
Elevation: 7,260-9,001 feet.
Maps: Gila National Forest, Twin Sisters 7.5-minute USGS quad.
Best season: Spring through fall.
Water availability: none.
Special attractions: tremendous views of Gila Wilderness and as far as the Chiricahua and Pinaleno Mountains of Arizona; thick conifer forest.

A fresh winter snow blankets Signal Peak.

HIKE 42 *SIGNAL PEAK*

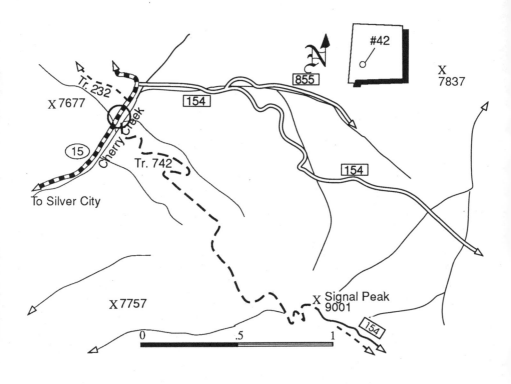

Finding the trailhead: Take State Highway 15 north from Silver City through the village of Pinos Altos. About four miles past Pinos Altos, the road passes the Ben Lilly Memorial and then enters Cherry Creek Canyon. The highway soon passes Cherry Creek and then McMillan Forest Campgrounds. The marked trail (742) takes off from the right side of the road about 1.5 miles past McMillan Campground. The Signal Peak road (154) turns off to the right only a couple of hundred yards further.

The hike: The Pinos Altos Range is the southernmost mountain range of the Gila Wilderness, the largest wilderness in New Mexico. Although this hike does not enter the wilderness area, great views of the wilderness greet hikers from the trail and the summit.

From its start on Highway 15, the trail crosses a meadow before starting its climb up into the forest covering the flanks of Signal Peak. Initially the trail passes through thick stands of Douglas fir on the moister north slopes of the mountain. As it climbs, it curves around onto the sunnier, drier, south-facing slopes of the peak and ponderosa pine becomes more common. While most of the hike travels through dense forest, regular breaks in the trees give increasingly dramatic views, especially to the south and southwest.

From the summit, with its fire lookout tower, you can see 360 degrees. To the east, north, and west lie the endless mountains ranges of the 3.3 million-acre Gila National Forest.

To the south and southwest, desert basin and range country stretches far into Arizona and Mexico. Below lies sleepy Pinos Altos, site of a gold mining boom begun in 1859.

Little mining continues today in Pinos Altos, but other large mines near Silver City and Santa Rita still produce enormous amounts of copper and other metals every year.

The Gila National Forest covers a large unpopulated area of high country consisting of many interconnected mountain ranges. The Continental Divide meanders though the national forest for 170 miles and crosses the Pinos Altos Range only about a mile southeast of the summit of Signal Peak. The Continental Divide Trail is being developed in New Mexico as part a route planned from Canada to Mexico. Much of it will traverse the Gila National Forest.

You can return to the trailhead via the lookout tower road, but at seven miles, it is considerably longer than the trail.

HIKE 43 PUEBLO PARK

General description: An easy day hike into the little-known Blue Range Wilderness.

General location: About ninety-five miles northwest of Silver City.

Length: About four miles round trip.

Elevation: 6,150-5,920 feet.

Maps: Gila National Forest, Saliz Pass 7.5-minute USGS quad.

Best season: All year.

Water availability: Pueblo Park Spring (seasonal).

Special attractions: Solitude, bytownite crystals.

Finding the trailhead: From Silver City, drive about sixty-five miles north on US 180 to Glenwood. From Glenwood, continue north on US 180 for about 26.5 miles to the junction with FR 232. Turn left onto FR 232, marked with a Pueblo Park Campground sign. Follow the good gravel road 6.2 miles to the Pueblo Park Campground.

The hike: Pueblo Park is actually located in the Apache National Forest, but shows up on the Gila National Forest map. The 29,304-acre Blue Range Wilderness was created out of the New Mexico portion of the Blue Range Primitive Area. It adjoins the much larger Blue Range Primitive Area in Arizona. The rugged mountainous area is probably one of the least visited areas in either state. Trails don't even penetrate large sections of the wilderness and primitive areas. The eastern end of the famous Mogollon Rim of Arizona begins here.

W.S. Mountain Trail 43 starts right across the road from the campground. The campground is set in a peaceful park-like area, wooded with large ponderosas. Except in very dry years, a spring supplies a water source at the campground.

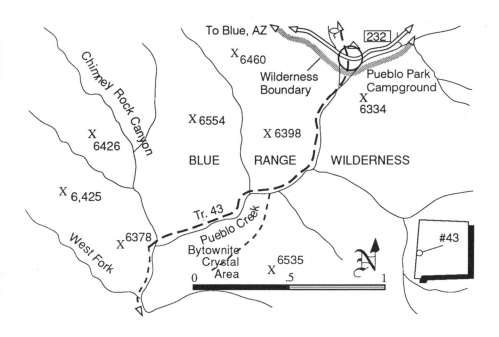

The hike is an easy walk down a scenic canyon, usually with some running water. The well-marked trailhead goes through a fence and immediately enters the wilderness. It quickly drops down off the bench into a rocky canyon bottom.

The trail is not obvious because floods periodically wash it out where it crosses the bottom. However, just follow the canyon bottom downstream and you'll pick it up again. Rock cairns and blazes occasionally help you find the way. Be sure to note where the trail first drops into the creek bottom so that you won't have trouble finding it on the way back.

The canyon quickly narrows and the walls steepen as the trail goes downstream. The trail crosses back and forth from side to side and travels on the narrow benches whenever possible. Don't worry if you lose the trail; it stays with the canyon for several miles. Generally, it's easier walking to follow the trail on the benches when possible. Ponderosas, alligator junipers, and cherry trees canopy much of the route.

Below about a mile, the stream usually runs with at least a small trickle.

Between about one mile and 1.5 miles, a faint trail climbs steeply several hundred feet up the left canyon wall onto a mesa top. Part of the mesa top is known for the occurence of semi-precious bytownite crystals. The clear, hard, pale yellow crystals are of good enough quality to cut and facet for jewelry. The small crystals lie loose on the ground, visible to the keen eye. If you can't find the side trail, don't worry. I've even found a few crystals simply by scrambling around on the left wall of the canyon after hiking a little more than a mile downstream from the trailhead.

At almost two miles, the canyon widens again where Chimney Rock Canyon flows in from the west. The large wooded bench at the confluence makes an excellent camp area at the end of the hike.

The easy trail continues almost three miles further down Pueblo Creek, before turning west up a major tributary, Bear Canyon. It continues for miles further, ultimately traveling far into Arizona. As with all warm weather hikes below 7,000 feet or so in elevation, keep an eye open for rattlesnakes, especially at dusk. An upset blacktail rattler that we didn't see in the dimness of twilight startled us as we neared the campground at the end of this hike. We gave him a wide berth and let him continue his evening hunt.

HIKE 44 *WHITEWATER CREEK*

General description: A moderate day hike into the Gila Wilderness via a spectacular rocky gorge.
General location: About seventy miles northwest of Silver City.
Length: About six miles round trip.
Elevation: 5,150-6,200 feet.
Maps: Gila Wilderness, Gila National Forest, Holt Mountain and Mogollon 7.5-minute USGS quads.
Best season: April through November.
Water availability: Whitewater Creek.
Special attractions: The "Catwalk," fall maples, permanent stream.
Finding the trailhead: From Silver City, drive northwest about sixty-five miles on US 180 to Glenwood. On the north side of the little village, turn right (east) on the marked turnoff (NM 174) to the Catwalk. Drive about five miles to the paved road's end at the Whitewater Picnic Ground.

The hike: The picnic area is located at the old townsite of Graham. The town was established in the late 1800s to mill ore taken from mines high in the mountains.

Floods have destroyed all but the mill foundations on the hillside above.

From the picnic ground, well-developed Trail 207 quickly enters a narrow rocky gorge. Parts of the trail follow steel catwalks suspended from the walls, with the rushing stream filling the canyon bottom below. Numerous bridges, large and small, criss-cross the creek. Here and there, the rusted remains of large pipes, iron bolts, and concrete foundations mark the old waterline used to feed the town and mill at Graham. The pipeline, built in 1893 and enlarged in 1897, was suspended high above the canyon bottom to avoid washouts, similar to the trail today. The narrow walkway on top of the pipe formed the first "catwalk" to repairmen.

The highly developed Catwalk trail ends under a large overhang above a waterfall. Trail 207 turns off to the left at the lower end of the suspension bridge right before the end of the developed trail. Look for the small "207"

Bigtooth maples, colorful in fall, line part of the south fork of Whitewater Creek.

sign bolted to the rock at the bridge. The trail climbs about 0.25 mile steeply upstream on the north side of the canyon to the junction with Trail 41, the Gold Dust Trail. Trail 41 forks sharply uphill to the left and goes to NM 159. It is used largely for Whitewater Creek access by horses, who are unable to use the Catwalk Trail.

The trail stays on the north side of the canyon all the way to the junction with the South Fork. Originally the trail followed the creek bottom, requiring several stream crossings and subject to washouts. Unfortunately, the Forest Service did a poor job of trail design when they relocated it on the north wall to avoid flood damage. Rather than following a continuous mild grade, the trail climbs steeply up the hillside and then drops down to the creek multiple times in the next mile. Although the overall elevation gain for the hike is not excessive, the continuous ups and downs add greatly to the effort required.

Although the absolute elevation of the hike is relatively low, the deep canyon cuts into the heart of the massive Mogollon Range, with peaks reaching almost 11,000 feet. Hence the creek is well-wooded with ponderosa, Douglas fir, sycamore, and other trees. At about 2.25 miles, the south fork of the creek joins the main canyon from the right. Turn right at the sign, and take South Fork Trail 212 across the creek and into the South Fork. At the junction are the foundations of the old power plant used to generate electricity for the mines

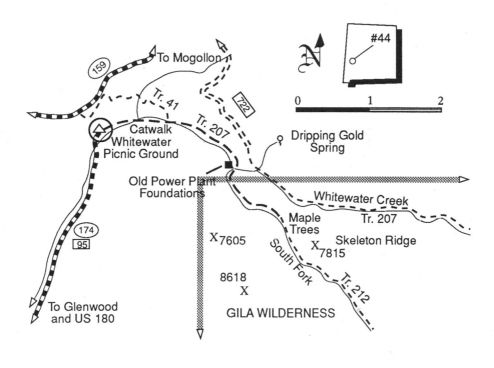

at the ghost town of Mogollon. The wooded level area at the junction provides several good campsites.

From the junction, the trail climbs steadily along the creek in the bottom of a narrower canyon. The tiring up and down of Trail 207 is left behind. At about 0.5 mile from the junction, the trail passes a large bench ideal for camping. Just beyond the bench, the trail enters a very narrow inner gorge where the trail and creek both try to occupy the same space. Just the other side of the short, mossy-walled gorge, the trail reaches the first good stands of bigtooth maples. The trail passes through the maples for some distance, before continuing miles further into the high wilderness country. Try to do the hike in mid-October when the maples turn glorious shades of gold and scarlet.

HIKE 45 *MOGOLLON BALDY*

General description: A moderate two to three day backpack to a remote mountaintop fire lookout in the heart of the Gila Wilderness.
General location: About eighty-five miles northwest of Silver City.
Length: About twenty-four miles round trip
Elevation:9,132-10,770 feet.
Maps: Gila Wilderness, Gila National Forest, Grouse Mountain, and Mogollon Baldy Peak 7.5-minute USGS quads.
Best season: Mid-May through October.
Water availability: Bead, Hummingbird, Apache, Hobo, Little Hobo, and Blacktail Springs.
Special attractions: Lush high mountain forest, spectacular views, isolation.
Finding the trailhead: From Silver City, drive about sixty-five miles northwest on US 180 to Glenwood. From Glenwood, drive about 3.7 miles north on US 180 to the junction with paved NM 159. Turn right and follow the steep, winding mountain road to the old mining ghost town of Mogollon. A few escapees from civilization are bringing new life to the picturesque town. The pavement ends in Mogollon, but a good all-weather gravel surface continues to and past the trailhead. After the first snows, the road is closed beyond Mogollon until late spring. From Mogollon, the road continues to climb up into forest thickly wooded with Douglas fir and aspen. Stop at the marked Sandy Point trailhead, approximately 18.2 miles from the turnoff at US 180.

The hike: This hike follows the crest of the Mogollon Range, the highest range in not only the Gila Wilderness, but all of southern New Mexico except Sierra Blanca many miles east. Most of the hike lies above 10,000 feet, so prepare to do a little heavy breathing. The Sandy Point trailhead is probably the most commonly used access to the high country, but is still rarely crowded.

The Gila Wilderness contains 558,065 acres, making it the largest in New Mexico. The wilderness lies in the heart of a rugged mountainous area that covers several million acres of southwestern New Mexico and stretches far into Arizona. The Gila forms the oldest wilderness area in the United States, having been set aside in 1924. Congress made the designation permanent in 1964 for the Gila Wilderness and many other areas. The headwaters of much of the Gila River start high in the Mogollon Range. The large mountain area supports healthy populations of deer, elk, bear, mountain lion, and other wildlife.

Be sure to take warm clothes and rain gear, especially in late summer when the rainy season is in full swing. Since the trail follows the crest of the range, it doesn't go near any creeks. Fortunately, however, the trail does pass several springs, making it unnecessary to carry large quantities of water. Before driving up the mountain from Glenwood, check at the Forest Service ranger station about the status of the various spings along the route. I last did the hike at the end of an extended drought, and Bead, Hummingbird, and Apache Springs were still all flowing well. Hobo and Little Hobo were very low, however, with only a small quantity of somewhat stagnant water. I did not visit Blacktail Spring. Be sure to treat your water before using.

The well-marked, well-maintained Trail 182 is easy to follow. It immediately begins climbing at a moderate grade from Sandy Point, passing some of the largest Douglas firs I have ever seen in the Southwest. At about 1.5 miles the trail's grade lessens and it crosses into the wilderness.

Shortly afterwards, the marked side trail to Bead Spring goes downhill to the left. The reliable, strongly flowing spring is only about 500 feet down the trail. Be careful not to trample the lush ferns, mosses, and other delicate vegetation at the spring. Huge aspens are mixed in with the spruce at the spring. After Bead Spring, most of the rest of the hike consists of relatively small ups and downs along the crest.

The trail maintains a very easy grade for the next 1.5 miles. Then a short, moderate climb brings the trail to a high point before dropping down slightly to Hummingbird Saddle. At about four miles out, the forest opens up for a short distance, giving a great view of the Whitewater Creek drainage below and far out into Arizona. Hummingbird Saddle, at about 4.75 miles, is a popular camping area because of many possible level sites and the nearby Hummingbird Spring. It also makes a good destination for day hikers. The spring is a few hundred yards down below the saddle to the right (west). A marked trail leads to it. The trail, 207, continues on past the spring to Redstone Park and all the way down Whitewater Creek (See Hike 44). Whitewater Baldy, the highest point in the Mogollon Range, rises right above the south side of the saddle. A faint, unofficial trail follows the crest from the saddle up to the summit. A bare area on its south side allows great views.

At all the trail junctions, just follow the signs to Mogollon Baldy. Usually the distances shown aren't exactly right, but they're close enough. The Forest Service hasn't generally marked the trail numbers on the signs, but Trail 182 is the route all the way to Mogollon Baldy.

From Hummingbird Saddle, Trail 182 drops slightly for the next mile or so. At about 5.5 miles (about 0.75 miles from the saddle), marked Trail 172 forks off to the left, to Iron Creek Lake (See Hike 46). Stay right, towards Baldy. In another 0.75 mile or so, the trail reaches another saddle on the crest. The level area makes an ideal campsite, although there is no close water source. The trail then climbs back up some, reaching the junction with Trail 181 at about 7.25 miles. Plentiful campsites exist in the crest area around the junction. The marked righthand trail goes to Spruce Creek Saddle and many other destinations. Apache Spring and possible campsites lie about 1.5 miles out on Trail 181. To continue on to Baldy, follow the sign onto the lefthand fork.

The trail begins to descend a short distance beyond the trail 181 junction. At a little more than eight miles, marked Trail 102 climbs steeply off to the left to Turkeyfeather Pass. Bear right to Baldy. Hobo Spring is next to the trail on the right about 0.5 mile beyond the Turkeyfeather Pass junction. A small area has been leveled out for camping near the spring. Check with the Forest Service about the spring's status before you start your hike. Little Hobo Spring is on the left side of the trail another 0.5 mile down the way.

At about ten miles, the trail reaches West Fork Saddle. At about 9600 feet, it is the lowest point on the hike other than the start of the trail at Sandy Point. The saddle has several excellent, level campsites. Trail 224 to Mogollon Creek forks down to the right from the saddle. The last two miles (1.5 miles according to the sign) to Baldy make up the longest sustained climb of the hike, gaining over 1,100 feet.

Blacktail Spring is to the left of the trail a little below the summit.

The summit commands tremendous views of not only the Gila Wilderness, but of mountains over much of southern New Mexico and Arizona. So much of the hike passes through dense woods that the views from the treeless summit are breathtaking in contrast. Such a large area surrounding the peak is undeveloped that virtually no sign of man is visible as far as the eye can see. The Forest Service, being aware of the peak's prominent summit, long ago built a fire lookout and ranger cabin on the summit. The lookout is manned from May through August. The facilities are for Forest Service use only, but the rangers usually enjoy visiting with hikers.

Camping is allowed on the summit, but not in the immediate vicinity of the tower and cabin. Be sure to pick up water on the way up; the rangers' supply on the summit is extremely limited. Please don't disturb the Forest Service facilities if the rangers aren't in residence. Believe it or not, even here vandals have struck.

Lightning is a threat along most of the crest trail, but is particularly dangerous on the bare summit of Mogollon Baldy. Thunderstorms can build within minutes in the mountains, especially in late summer afternoons. If you get wet, hypothermia is also a danger. While early summer is usually the dryest time of year for hiking in the Mogollons, the mountains look their lush green best in August. Even here in southern New Mexico, patches of snow can cover the trail as late as early June in good snow years. I day hiked up Whitewater Baldy on Memorial Day weekend one year and had to push through drifts for much of the last half of the hike.

Check with the Forest Service for current conditions.

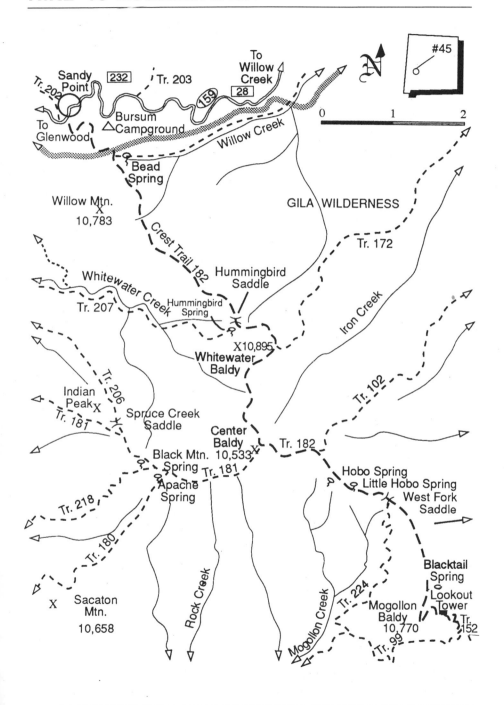

HIKE 46 *IRON CREEK*

General description: An easy day hike to one of many permanent streams in the Gila Wilderness.

General location: About ninety-five miles northwest of Silver City.

Length: About five miles round trip.

Elevation: 7,880-8,330 feet..

Maps: Gila Wilderness, Gila National Forest, Negrito Mountain 7.5-minute USGS quad.

Best season: May through October.

Water availability: Iron Creek.

Special attractions: Trout stream, lush forest.

Finding the trailhead: Follow the same directions as those for Hike 45. However, take NM 159 for 27.2 miles from US 180, instead of the 18.2 miles directed in Hike 45.

This road is usually closed from the first snow to late spring. The trailhead is usually accessible for a somewhat longer season by using FR 141 from Reserve. At 27.2 miles turn right onto FR 507, the Willow Creek Campground turnoff.

Go 0.2 mile down FR 507 to a small dirt road on the left marked with a Forest Trail 151 sign (just past the campground entrance). Turn onto it and cross Willow Creek. Go left in about 0.1 mile at an unmarked fork. The road ends at the trailhead in about 100 yards.

The hike: Trail 151 is one of the more heavily used trailheads in the enormous Gila Wilderness. However, as with most of the Gila area, "heavily used" does not usually signify great numbers of people. The area is just too remote to receive large numbers of visitors. The nearest cities of any size, Albuquerque and El Paso, are over 200 miles away.

Even Silver City, with less than 20,000 people, is almost 100 miles away. Catron County, in which much of the wilderness is located, is the largest county in New Mexico with about 8,000 square miles, but has less than 3,000 people. This hike is an introduction to the heavily forested middle-elevation area of the wilderness. Many of the trails in the Willow Creek area are characteristically long, but easy, with only moderate elevation changes.

From the marked trailhead, the well-maintained route goes about 150 yards up a small tributary of Willow Creek, before turning left and crossing the little stream. A short fork to the right goes only to a corral and storage shed. Just across the creek, signs mark the trail and wilderness boundary. The trail climbs up the hillside, overlooking the Willow Creek valley. It then turns southerly up a small drainage and away from Willow Creek.

The trail passes through lush stands of Douglas fir as it climbs up the small drainage to the top of a relatively flat mesa top. The trail passes through heavy ponderosa pine, until it meets the junction with Trail 172 on the right at Iron Creek Lake. Trail 172 climbs up to Whitewater Baldy and Hummingbird Saddle (See Hike 45). Stay left on Trail 151 as it goes around the lake, a shallow, marshy pond with water levels dependent on precipitation. Just past the lake, Trail 171 splits off to the left, going to the Middle Fork of the Gila River and Snow

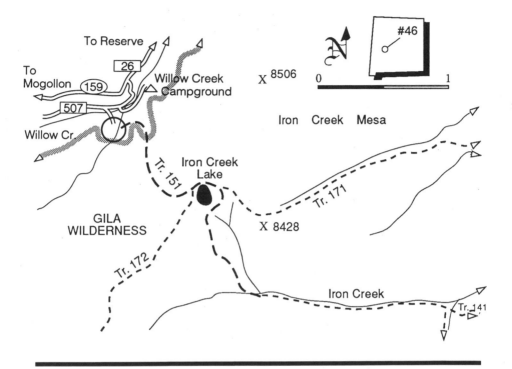

Lake. Trail 171, combined with Trail 157, makes a long, but not too difficult loop back to Willow Creek. However, stay right on Trail 151 to Iron Creek.

From the junction, the trail stays relatively level for some distance before dropping down into a small drainage that leads into Iron Creek. At about 2.5 miles from the start, the trail reaches Iron Creek and turns downstream. The permanent stream tumbles down from the high crest of the Mogollon Range through lush forest. As with most of the permanent streams of the Gila Wilderness, trout thrive in the cold mountain waters.

The hike can easily be extended by following Trail 151 further downstream. A large overnight loop can be created by following 151 to Trail 141. Go left on 141, then left again on 175 at its intersection. Finally return to Willow Creek by going left on either Trail 171 or 157 from Trail 175.

HIKE 47 *GILA CLIFF DWELLINGS*

General description: An very easy hike up to the ancient ruins of Gila Cliff Dwellings National Monument.
General location: About forty-five miles north of Silver City.
Length: About one mile round trip.
Elevation:5,700-5880 feet.
Maps: Gila Cliff Dwellings brochure, Little Turkey Park 7.5-minute USGS quad.
Best season: All year.
Water availability: Trailhead.
Special attractions: Ancient dwellings.
Finding the trailhead: Take NM 15 from Silver City about forty-five miles north to the end of the road at Gila Cliff Dwellings National Monument.

No one is sure why residents abandoned Gila Cliff Dwellings almost 700 years ago.

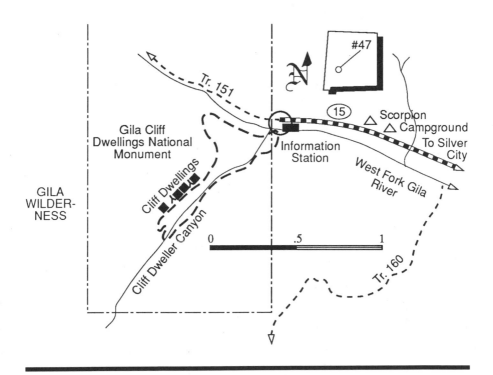

The hike: The easy hike climbs up to a series of seven natural caves, five of which contain the ruins of cliff dwellings. The buildings were constructed sometime after 1000 AD, along with other pueblos built in the open on terraces above the Gila River's West Fork. The Pueblo people who lived here farmed the flood plain and mesa tops, raising corn, beans, and squash. Hunting and gathering supplemented their diet. Sometime in the early 1300s, they abandoned their homes and left. Archaeologists have not been able to determine why with any certainty.

The caves protected the ruins from the elements, leaving them much better preserved than those built in the open. About forty rooms were built in the caves using stone and timber. All of the wood remaining in the dwellings are original.

From the parking lot at the end of NM 15, the trail crosses a bridge over the West Fork and enters a small, narrow canyon. The trail criss-crosses the wooded canyon's usually permanent small stream, before climbing 180 feet up to the dwellings. At the ruins, the trail goes in and out of the caves, through the old buildings. The loop trail then descends back to the trailhead by a different route.

The ruins trail is open all year except Christmas and New Year's Day. The hours vary seasonally, so call ahead for current times. NM Highway 15 from Silver City is narrow, steep, and winding; allow two hours to drive it.

HIKE 48 *GILA WEST FORK*

General description: An easy hike up the West Fork of the Gila River into the Gila Wilderness.

General location: About forty-five miles north of Silver City.

Length: About six miles round trip.

Elevation:5,700-5,790 feet.

Maps: Gila Wilderness, Gila National Forest, Little Turkey Park 7.5-minute USGS quad.

Best season: All year.

Water availability: Gila River.

Special attractions: Rugged gorge, beaver dams, cliff dwelling.

Finding the trailhead: Take NM 15 from Silver City about forty-five miles north to the end of the road at Gila Cliff Dwellings National Monument.

The hike: The Gila River, especially the west and middle forks, drains large areas of the immense Gila Wilderness. With over one-half million acres, the wilderness is by far the largest in New Mexico. The long, winding drive to the Gila Cliff Dwellings gives some idea of the size of the unpopulated mountainous area. Even though the road is paved, allow two hours to traverse the steep, narrow highway.

The trail starts at the Gila Cliff Dwellings parking lot at the end of the road. The trailhead is one of the most popular entry points into the Gila Wilderness but is still rarely crowded. The size of the wilderness and the multitude of possible trails quickly dilutes the density of hikers. This hike is an easy day hike up the river, serving as an introduction to the lower part of the wilderness. This trail and others can be easily followed thirty miles or more without hitting another road.

The trail starts up the north side of the broad river bottom. Cottonwoods, willows, and ash trees cover the floodplain. Even though the elevation is relatively low, the surrounding mountains attract more rain than is typical for this elevation in New Mexico. Thus, ponderosas, mixed with pinyon and juniper, grow on the hillsides. The river is a permanent, broad stream that can be difficult to ford with dry feet even at its lowest levels. During spring snow melt and late summer rains, the river is often high enough to make dry crossings impossible. Because of the multiple river crossings, I recommend that you carry an extra pair of old tennis shoes, especially on overnight trips. Be aware of the weather, even miles away. The Gila occasionally has severe floods.

After passing some beaver dams, the trail crosses into the wilderness at about 0.5 mile. About 0.5 mile further, the trail makes its first crossing to the south bank and climbs onto a low bench. The level, ponderosa-covered bench is ideal for camping. On the bench a marked trail forks off to the left to Little Creek. Stay right, along the river to Hells Hole. The river valley begins to narrow into a rocky canyon.

About 0.75 mile from the trail junction, the trail drops off the bench and crosses back to the north side of the river.

Just across the river, the trail forks again. The marked trail to The Meadows

HIKE 48 GILA WEST FORK

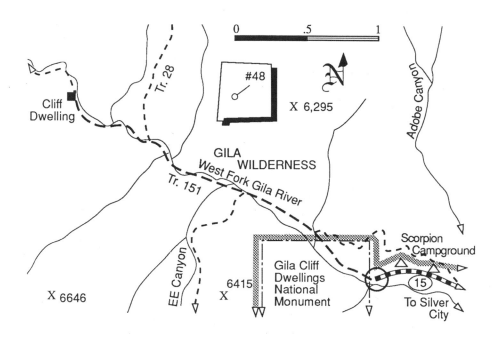

goes right and climbs out of the canyon. Bear left and stay with the river trail toward Hells Hole.

After the trail junction, the river trail gets rocky, somewhat overgrown, and hard to follow for a couple of hundred yards. Just follow the river and you'll find it again. The canyon begins to really narrow and deepen, with sheer rocky walls. The trail starts to criss-cross the river frequently, with one stretch climbing well up the south bank. At a sharp bend in the river, a little less than three miles from the trailhead, the canyon becomes a spectacular rocky chasm. High on the walls are arches and caves. On the left wall an ancient cliff dwelling rests in a small cave. It's best not to try to climb up to it. The route is a dangerous scramble above a cliff, and erosion created by visitation is causing the the ruin's walls to collapse. Enjoy the rocky gorge just beyond the cliff dwelling before returning the same way.

HIKE 49 *MIMBRES RIVER*

General description: A moderate dayhike or overnight trip along the Mimbres River in the Aldo Leopold Wilderness.

General location: About fifty miles northeast of Silver City.

Length: About thirteen miles round trip.

Elevation: 6940-7675 feet.

Maps: Gila National Forest, Aldo Leopold Wilderness, Hay Mesa 7.5-minute USGS quad.

Best season: April through December.

Water availability: Mimbres River.

Special attractions: Mountain stream, solitude, forest.

Finding the trailhead: From Silver City, drive about eight miles east on US 180 to Central. Turn left on NM 152 and drive about 14.4 miles east to NM 35. Turn left and follow NM 35 about 15.2 miles north to NM 61, the Wall Lake turnoff. Turn right on gravel NM 61. If you had any doubt that you were entering a remote area, read the sign: "Road Ahead Restricted—Four Wheel Drive and High Axle Vehicle." This is a state highway? Another sign says: "No Food, Lodging, or Gasoline Next 120 Miles." Don't worry; you're stopping short of the bad stretch of road.

Follow NM 61/FR 150, a good all-weather gravel road, for about 7.3 miles to the marked FR 150A turnoff to Cooney and the Mimbres River on the right. The road crosses North Star Mesa, where the forest has been practically clearcut by firewood cutters. The dry, slow-growing southwestern forests used for firewood cutting are not a renewable resource with the current large human population. Turn right onto FR 150A.

The first 0.7 mile is very good and the next 0.7 mile down to the river is steep, but usually passable by any vehicle.

Cross the river and continue up the canyon to the end of the road at a ranch house at 2.8 miles. Park outside the fence surrounding the ranch house.

The hike: The Black Range is long, stretching almost 100 miles from north to south along a high crest. Several peaks along the crest top out at over 10,000 feet. The mountains make up a major component of the enormous 3.3-million-acre Gila National Forest. Most of the mountains are accessible only by horse or foot, with the heart protected by the 202,000-acre Aldo Leopold Wilderness. The heavily forested range is criss-crossed with several hundred miles of trails, most little, if ever, used. The very long trails are ideal for multi-day backpacking trips.

The almost undiscovered mountains make an great place to lose yourself, far from civilization. This trail was chosen because it is usually accessible by any vehicle and it follows along one of the range's permanent streams. It's one of the most popular entry points into the Aldo Leopold Wilderness, but don't worry, it's all relative. You still probably won't see but a handful of people on the trail.

From the parking area in front of the ranch house, hike up the rough road to the right along the fence and around the house. Don't cut through the yard; it's private property.

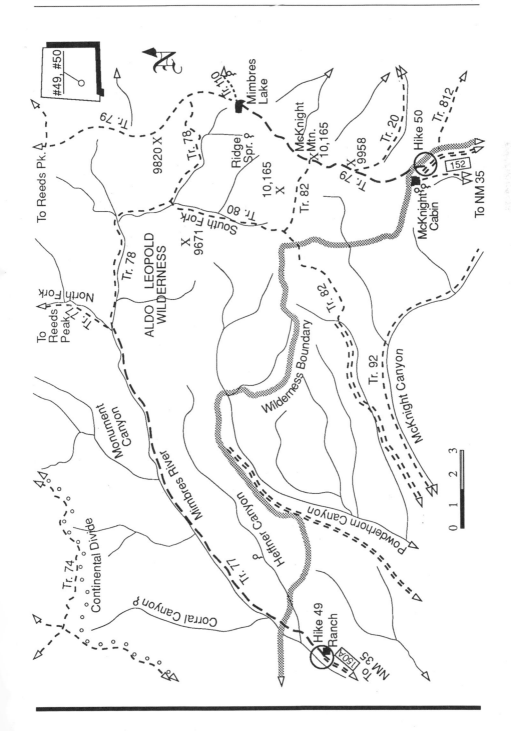

Trail 77 goes upstream, skirting the ranch on the slopes above, before rejoining the river. A sign marks the trailhead in front of the house, but it was in bad shape when I last visited. It says that Mimbres Lake is 11.75 miles and Reeds Peak is 12.25 miles.

The trail is excellent, smooth and well-maintained. The hiking is easy; I gave this hike a moderate rating only because of its length. Most of the first part of the hike is in open ponderosa and cottonwood forest. The trail enters the wilderness area a bit less than one mile up canyon. Shortly afterward you hit the first of many stream crossings. The Mimbres River is really more of a stream than a river, except in flood. However, it's still large enough to be a nuisance to cross. In early spring and late summer, plan on getting your feet wet and don't worry about trying to find a dry crossing point. Take an extra pair of shoes if you're backpacking. Many beautiful campsites lie all along the hike. Camp well away from the stream and trail.

At about three miles, in a park-like area of ponderosa pine in a broad part of the canyon, you will pass an old corral. Shortly afterward, you will hit lush patches of Douglas fir and aspen mixed in with the ponderosa. At about five miles, another even more deteriorated corral is passed. At about 6.5 miles, at the end of this hike, the trail forks. To the left, according to the sign, lies Reeds Peak 5.75 miles away on Trail 77 and to the right lies Mimbres Lake 5.25 miles away on Trail 78. The Mimbres River also forks, with Trail 77 following the North Fork and Trail 78 following the Middle Fork.

For a tremendous three-day backpacking trip, follow Trail 78 up to Mimbres Lake (see Hike 50), take Crest Trail 79 north to Reeds Peak, and return via Trail 77 to the fork at the end of this hike.

HIKE 50 *MIMBRES LAKE*

General description: A moderate day hike to a small, marshy, natural pond in the Aldo Leopold Wilderness.
General location: About fifty miles northeast of Silver City.
Length: About seven miles round trip.
Elevation: 9,560-10,165 feet.
Maps: Gila National Forest, Aldo Leopold Wilderness, Victoria Park 7.5-minute UGGS quad.
Best season: May through November.
Water availability: See text—Mimbres Lake, Ridge Spring, North Seco Spring, McKnight Cabin Spring.
Special attractions: Small pond, lush forest, views, solitude.
Finding the trailhead: From Silver City, take US 180 about eight miles east to Central. Turn left onto NM 152 and continue east about 14.4 miles to NM 35. Turn left and go north on NM 35 about 12.3 miles the marked McKnight Road (FR 152). Follow FR 152 about 17.4 miles up onto the crest of the Black Range. Park at the Trail 79 sign. The end of the road is only 0.3 mile further at the McKnight Cabin. FR 152 is an excellent gravel road for about the first nine miles to the junction of FR 537. After this point a high-clearance vehicle is recommended to negotiate the rocks and ruts. I made it to the top in a sedan,

Mimbres Lake is a small marshy natural lake in the Aldo Leopold Wilderness.

but I would only recommend it for short wheelbase sedans with very able drivers. Check with the Forest Service in advance.

The hike: This hike starts on the crest of the Black Range and is one of the most scenic hikes in the mountains.

Much of the heart of the range is protected by the enormous Aldo Leopold Wilderness. This trail enters the wilderness area almost immediately. Most of the mountains have never had much impact from the activities of man. Even today, the extensive mountain range is relatively undiscovered, making it unlikely that you will see many people. Most people who actually make it to this corner of New Mexico head for the better-known Gila Wilderness.

The hike can easily be done as a dayhike, but begs to be done as a two or three day trip. If you are doing more than a dayhike, be sure to check on the status of the springs and lake before starting. Usually water can be found at at least some of the sources, but you need to know ahead of time. Water is usually available at McKnight Cabin Spring by the corral just below the cabin at the end of the road.

The trail starts out by heading straight into an aspen grove. The sign at the trailhead, saying "Mimbres Lake 4.5" miles, is wrong; it's about 3.5 miles. The trail is somewhat more difficult than the elevations and length indicate because it climbs up over a couple of mountains before reaching the lake, which lies at almost the same elevation as the trailhead. The trail quickly begins climbing. At about 0.3 mile, an unmarked trail forks downhill to the left, going to the cabin. The trail then climbs steeply to the top of a flat-topped, unnamed summit.

The trail then drops down to a saddle in the crest, passing in and out of young aspen stands. The next 1.5 miles follow the narrow crest, giving great views both east and west. The young aspens and frequent views are the result of the 40,000-acre McKnight fire in the 1950s. The maps show Trail 20 as forking off to the right, but I didn't see it. Many Black Range trails are disappearing from lack of use.

At about 1.5 miles, the trail begins the steep climb up McKnight Mountain, gaining about 500 feet. The top is reached at about two miles. A fifty-yard, marked side trail on the right takes you to the rocky summit. Be sure to climb up and enjoy the 360-degree views from the highest point in the Black Range. You'll see endless miles of mountains with almost no sign of man.

Just past the summit, marked Trail 82 forks uphill to the left to FR 151. Go downhill to the right toward Mimbres Lake.

The observant will notice that the rest of the trail appears to follow what was once a four-wheel drive road many years ago. The trail leaves the old burned area and descends steeply for a short distance off of the peak. The trail now passes through dense fir and spruce forest on a broader, flatter portion of the crest. At about three miles, a drainage is passed on the left, down which lies Ridge Spring. I did not visit the spring, although a faint trail appeared to lead down the drainage toward it.

Just before reaching the lake, hikers will notice an enormous Douglas fir on the right side of the trail. The tree is probably the largest tree of any kind that I have seen in New Mexico. It appeared to be about seven feet in diameter at chest height and towered high up in the canopy.

The shallow, marshy Mimbres Lake lies in a beautiful level clearing, surrounded by a dense forest of spruce, fir, and aspen. I dayhiked to the lake and regretted not being able to camp. Be sure to find a site well away from the lake to avoid polluting it or scaring away wildlife. Innumerable campsites exist in the large, level mountaintop area around the lake. The area would make a great base camp for dayhikes along the Crest Trail and side trails. Marked Trail 110 forks off of Trail 79 at the lake. Although I did not visit it, the map indicates North Seco Spring as lying about 0.5 mile down Trail 110. Ridge Spring or North Seco Spring would probably make better water sources than the marshy lake. If all are dry, try walking down the Mimbres River on Trail 78 until the stream appears (see map).

A tremendous three-day backpack could be done by following Trail 79 to Reeds Peak and looping back to the lake via Trails 77 and 78. See the map and the description of Hike 49 for ideas.

HIKE 51 *HILLSBORO PEAK*

General description: A moderate day hike to a lookout tower on one of the high peaks of the Black Range.
General location: About forty miles east of Silver City.
Length: About ten miles round trip.
Elevation: 8,166-10,011 feet.
Maps: Gila National Forest, Aldo Leopold Wilderness, Hillsboro Peak 7.5-minute USGS quad.
Best season: May through November.
Water availability: Hillsboro Spring—see text.
Special attractions: Views, forest.
Finding the trailhead: From Silver City, drive about eight miles east on US 180 to Central. Turn left onto NM 152 and continue east about thirty-two miles to the trailhead at the top of Emory Pass. From I-25 to the east, drive west on NM 152 past Hillsboro and Kingston to Emory Pass at the top of the Black Range.

The hike: The Black Range stretches almost 100 miles from north to south, west of the Rio Grande Valley. The Continental Divide follows the crest along the north end of the range. The rugged mountains have less people in them now than at the turn of the century. Mining towns in the foothills boomed in the 1880s: Kingston, Hillsboro, and Lake Valley on the southeast side below Hillsboro Peak and Winston and Chloride on the northeast. Lake Valley had one of the most famous mining discoveries in the West. A single underground room, the "Bridal Chamber," contained over three million dollars of pure silver. The metal was so easy to mine that it was loaded directly onto railroad cars. Today, the mines have closed and the saloons have disappeared, leaving the communities to slumber peacefully in the New Mexico sun. The mountains towering over the towns now contain one of New Mexico's largest wildernesses and are almost forgotten.

When you do this hike, be sure to spend a little time in Kingston and Hillsboro, just down NM 152 from the trailhead. The sleepy little villages, with their old buildings and apple orchards, invite exploration. Paved NM 152 winds over the crest of the southern end of the mountains and provides the easiest access to Black Range trails. The trails leading from the pass are probably the most popular in the mountains, but are still relatively lightly used. You will probably only see people on summer weekends. Several nice campgrounds lie along NM 152, just down the west side of the pass.

Park at Emory Pass Vista, located just off the highway at the pass. Well-marked Trail 79 starts about 200 feet up the short paved side road that leads to the vista parking lot.

The well-maintained trail immediately begins climbing to the north from the road. Just up the way, you hit a dirt road. The short road just leads from the highway to some Forest Service facilities. Turn right and follow it uphill a short distance, passing a building, heliport, and radio tower. Go through a gate and follow the old, unused road, now the trail.

A fire lookout tower caps the flat summit of Hillsboro Peak.

About 200 yards past the gate, the old road is blocked off. The trail drops below and parallel to the abandoned road before rejoining it in about 0.25 mile.

The trail passes through Douglas fir and ponderosa, alternating with patches of oak scrub that have grown up after an old fire. Open areas provide great views as you follow the crest north. At about two miles, you hit the Aldo Leopold Wilderness boundary, marked by a small sign. The rest of the trail roughly follows the edge of the wilderness. At a little over three miles, the trail hits a well-marked four-way intersection. A large sign formally announces the wilderness. To the right, little-used Trail 127 descends six miles to Kingston, a nice hike with a car shuttle. To the left goes the more popular Hillsboro Peak Bypass Trail 412.

Trail 412 makes a good cutoff for early season hikers wanting to continue north along the crest. Trail 79, up on the north side of the peak, retains snow until later in the spring.

Continue straight ahead, uphill, on Trail 79 to the summit.

An unmarked trail forks off to the right, descending into Mineral Creek, about 0.5 mile up Trail 79 from the intersection. Like many Black Range trails, it's faint and almost unused. You probably won't even notice it.

Another unmarked, but much more obvious intersection is reached just short of the summit. The right fork is Trail 117. Stay left and climb the last fifty

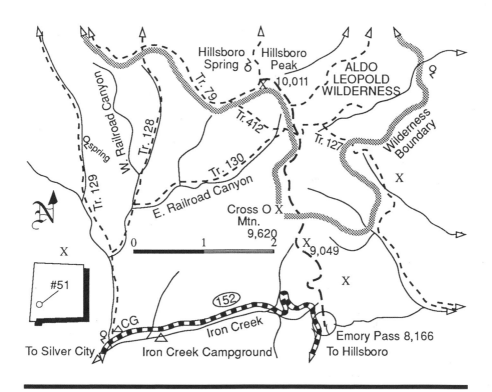

yards or so onto the large, flat summit at just less than five miles. A tall lookout tower and some Forest Service buildings are clustered at one side of the summit. The tower is occupied in the fire season of late spring and early summer. Please don't disturb any of the facilities. The views from the summit, and especially the tower, are tremendous. On a clear day, the view stretches from Sierra Blanca in southeastern New Mexico to mountains in southeastern Arizona.

Since much of the trail, and the summit in particular, are exposed to lightning, start your hike early in the day. Good campsites can be found on several saddles along the way and on the summit (but not too close to the buildings). Hillsboro Spring lies below the summit to the northwest off of Trail 117. I didn't visit the spring, so ask the Forest Service ahead of time about its status and exact location. For a good two-day hike with a car shuttle, continue north on Trail 79 to Trail 128. Turn left on Trail 128 and follow it down Railroad Canyon to Trail 129 in Gallinas Canyon. Continue down Trail 129 to NM 152. The hike can be enlarged by continuing further along Trail 79 to Trail 129 and following it all the way down Gallinas Canyon to NM 152. The Black Range has miles and miles of empty trails to explore. Use this hike as an introduction. If more people don't use some of these trails, the Forest Service will probably abandon them.

HIKE 52 *SAWYERS PEAK*

General description: A moderate day hike to a southern peak of the Black Range.
General location: About forty miles east of Silver City.
Length: About eight miles round trip.
Elevation: 8,166-9668 feet.
Maps: Gila National Forest, Hillsboro Peak and Maverick Mountain 7.5-minute USGS quads.
Best season: May through November.
Water availability: None.
Special attractions: Views, lush forest, solitude.
Finding the trailhead: Follow the same directions as Hike 51, Hillsboro Peak. Park in the gravel lot right on the highway at the pass, rather than in the Emory Pass Vista parking area.

The hike: Like the Hillsboro Peak hike, the Sawyers Peak trail is easily accessible from NM 152 at Emory Pass. The trail is one of the more popular trails in the Black Range, but "popular" is relative. Some trails near Santa Fe and Albuquerque probably get more visitors on a summer weekend than Sawyers Peak gets all year. This trail follows the crest of the Black Range south from NM 152. The bulk of the mountains lie to the north of the highway, but the smaller southern section is very scenic and little-visited.

The southern end doesn't lie in a formal wilderness, unlike much of the central and northern parts, but still has all the trappings.

Trail 79 climbs southwest from the gravel parking lot. A trail sign marks the start. The well-maintained trail climbs at a moderate grade on or near the crest for most of the hike. Unlike Hillsboro or McKnight Peak, the area around Sawyers Peak has not had any forest fires for many years. Because of the lack of fires and the trail's location on shady north-facing slopes for much of the way, lush forest lines almost the entire route. Broad views open up occasionally, but for the most part the trail winds through dense fir, spruce, aspen, and pine.

At a little over two miles, little-used Silver Creek Trail 146 forks off to the right. Stay left on Trail 79 and continue climbing. At about three miles, even less-used Trail 134 forks left down Trujillo Canyon. Continue to the right on trail 79 to Sawyers Peak. Finally, about 0.75 mile further on, you reach the base of the peak on the southeast side. At this point, Trail 79 begins to descend to the south, following the lowering crest of the mountains. Views start to open up to the south. The summit is reached by climbing back to the northwest on a short side trail up the crest through the trees. The rounded peak is heavily wooded, allowing few clear views. Better views lie just to the south of the peak along Trail 79.

The best campsites probably lie on the summit or along Trail 79 near the base of the summit. To leave any remaining people behind, just continue south along the Crest Trail. Very few people go beyond Sawyers Peak. Be sure to take topographic maps, since the trail gets faint in places. If a car shuttle can be arranged, an excellent hike would follow Trail 79 all the way to FR 886.

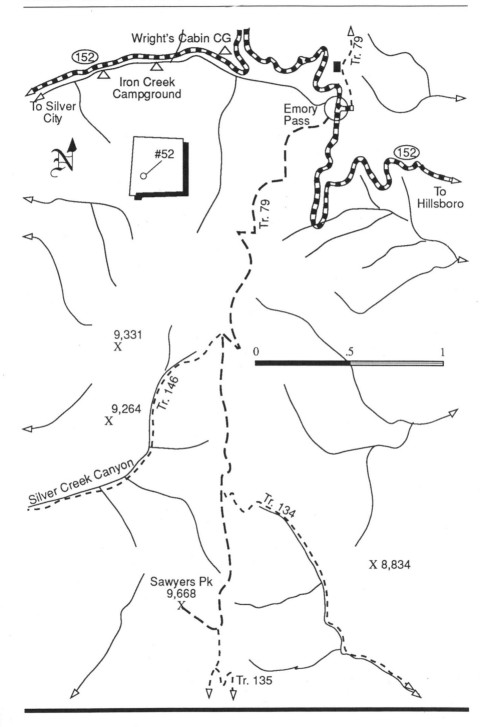

HIKE 53 *COOKS PEAK*

General description: A strenuous day hike to the craggy summit of Cooks Peak.
General location: About twenty-five miles north of Deming.
Length: About eleven miles round trip.
Elevation: 5,380-8,408 feet.
Maps: Gila National Forest, Lake Valley 15-minute or OK Canyon 7.5-minute USGS quads.
Best season: Spring and fall.
Water availability: Riley Spring—see text.
Special attractions: Solitude, ghost town, views.
Finding the trailhead: From I-25 in Deming, turn north on US 180 to Silver City. At about one mile, turn right on NM 26 toward Hatch. Go northeast on NM 26 for about 14.6 miles to an unmarked gravel road on the left. A lone ranch house is on the corner and a large old watertank is on the right. Follow the excellent county dirt road to the northwest toward prominent Cooks Peak. At about 5.1 miles, ignore the Hyatt Ranch road forking off to the left. At about 9.8 miles, the road hits a large dry desert wash. Ignore the rough road forking off to the left just before the wash. To this point the road is usually very good. The last 1.2 miles are rougher, but usually passable with a sedan if care is used. Recent storms usually determine the road condition. Carefully cross the wash, and drive to a locked gate at about eleven miles. A corral, a cottonwood, and BLM signs mark the spot.

The hike: Cooks (or Cookes) Peak towers above the southwestern New Mexico desert in splendid isolation, forming a landmark visible for many miles. The granite peak makes a distinctive rocky crag reminiscent of the Matterhorn. A series of low foothills connects the Cooks Range with the larger Black Range to the north. For centuries, the Apaches used the peak as a lookout. In the 1850s, the Butterfield Stage was routed by the peak to get water at several springs.

Frequent Indian raids led to the establishment of Fort Cummings at Cooks Spring in 1863. Lead-silver ore was discovered at the base of the peak in the 1870s and a small town was established along the route of the hike. The mines have long since played out and little remains of the townsite.

This hike initially follows an old road, but then climbs cross-country to the summit. The route is steep and strenuous and requires some scrambling up bare rock. Only expert hikers in good condition should attempt it. Except right after heavy snows, this hike can be done anytime of year. However, since this is mostly a desert hike, summers can be very hot. Winters are unpredictable. I climbed the peak in late December in a t-shirt, but colder weather is more normal. A topographic map and compass should be taken for this hike. Be sure to carry enough water; the springs may not be reliable.

Except for a few inholdings, most of the land around the peak is state- or BLM-owned. The fence at the locked gate says "No tresspassing" because the road runs through a small inholding. The BLM has established legal right of road access to the gate, but not beyond. Originally the landowner, Tom

Distant Cooks Peak rises above City of Rocks State Park.

Hyatt, did not lock the gate. However, he probably suffered vandalism or other problems from inconsiderate visitors.

Please respect private property. By calling Mr. Hyatt ahead of time, you might be able to obtain permission to drive through the gate, cutting two miles from the hike. However, the last two miles of road often require at least a high clearance vehicle for one of the wash crossings.

Although the Cooks Range is not in national forest, the Gila National Forest map shows the range in the lower righthand corner on the Silver City side. The map is useful for showing the private land inholdings. Assuming that you don't have permission to cross Hyatt's land, walk left (south) along the fence line to the large dry wash that you drove across a mile back down the road. Follow the wash upstream until you hit the road again in a short distance. Along the way, you'll pass fairly close to Shale Spring. Rejoin the road and follow it up the broad canyon. A little more than a mile up, you'll pass a windmill and the weathered, leaning crosses of the old cemetary on the left. At about two miles you will find the old townsite. Not much remains, other than scattered junk and an old rusting car. A couple of frame buildings still stand on the slope above, but probably not for much longer. At night, when the wind whistles and moans, you can almost hear the clink of whiskey bottles and the pounding of the stamp mills. Please don't disturb or remove what little is left. Riley Spring, if you can find it, is near the townsite.

HIKE 53 COOKS PEAK

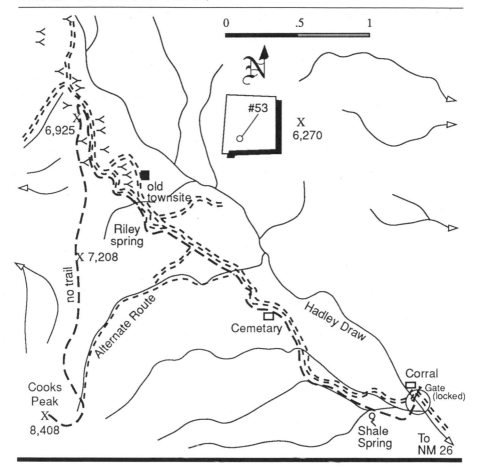

Continue to follow the old road northwest up the slope toward the mine workings and the ridge top. Be careful around the old mines. Open shafts are scattered across the ridge and the tunnels are unstable. At a little over three miles, the road reaches a saddle in the top of the ridge. Leave the road and cut back south, cross-country, toward the peak along the ridgetop.

The first 1.5 miles along the ridge aren't too difficult. The ridge doesn't climb too much and is relatively flat. You will encounter a few pinyons and junipers, which provide welcome shade. At about 4.5 miles, you will be at the base of the peak, although still about 1,200 feet below the summit.

Sheer cliffs crown most of the peak, so you must circle around the base to the east side as you climb. The last mile is by far the hardest part of the hike. Work your way southeast around the base into the upper end of the canyon below you to the left (east). Don't climb too high before you get to the upper end of the canyon, or you will find yourself having to cross several steep talus slopes below the cliffs. Don't venture onto the talus slopes. They are composed of larger rocks and boulders on a very unstable slope. Climb south up and out of the drainage to the ridgetop. Follow the ridgetop west to the summit. Pick your route carefully; although you will have to scramble up some rock at the end, there's no need to climb any cliffs.

If you achieve the summit, congratulations. Few people ever climb it. Chances are, you and the ghosts will have the entire mountain range to yourselves. Relax and enjoy one of the best views in New Mexico. You can descend the same way, or go all the way down the steep canyon that you climbed up near the top. Another way to shorten the distance is to cut straight down off the long approach ridge to the townsite, rather than following it all the way north back to the road.

Follow OK Canyon for a completely different route to Cooks Peak.

HIKE 54 *ICE CANYON*

General description: An easy day hike into a sheltered canyon on the west side of the Organ Mountains.
General location: About ten miles east of Las Cruces.
Length: About three miles round trip.
Elevation: 5,650-6,150 feet.
Maps: BLM brochure, Organ Peak 7.5-minute USGS quad.
Best season: Year round.
Water availability: Dripping Springs.
Special attractions: Sheltered steep-walled canyon; historic buildings.
Finding the trailhead: In Las Cruces, take the University exit off of Interstate 25 and turn east, up toward the mountains. The pavement quickly turns into a washboard gravel surface. At about four miles, the pavement returns for about one mile. When the pavement ends again, bear straight ahead back onto the gravel road. Don't turn right and follow the pavement. Follow the BLM Dripping Springs signs. Continue east-northeast. At about 10.5 miles, park at road's end at the A.B. Cox Visitor Center.

The hike: In the 1870s, Colonel Eugene Van Patten built a mountain resort at Dripping Springs. The resort was a popular escape from the heat of the Rio Grande Valley at the turn of the century. In 1917 the resort went bankrupt and was sold to Dr. Nathan Boyd, who converted it into a tuberculosis sanitorium. He built additional structures in the canyon to house his patients. Eventually the sanitorium closed and the buildings fell into disrepair.

Recently the Nature Conservancy bought part of the property to help protect endangered species found in the canyon, particularly the Organ Mountain primrose. The land was turned over to the BLM, but is jointly managed by volunteers from both organizations. The visitor center and canyon are only open for day use. Since the canyon is closed on certain weekdays, be sure to call either the visitor center or the BLM office in Las Cruces before making the drive up to the canyon.

From the visitor center, follow the trail signs up the old road. The road goes up the broad, mostly desert canyon floor.

At the ruined buildings of the old coach stop, the canyon starts to narrow and oak, juniper, and hackberry woodland starts to appear. The sheer canyon

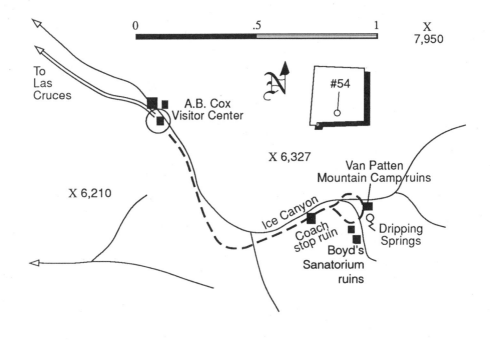

walls pull in closer and closer as the trail continues up. Near the end, the trail forks into a small loop. Go right up to some of the old buildings erected as part of Boyd's Sanitorium. Just around the loop from the sanitorium, the water of Dripping Springs drips off of cliffs above. In a pinch, water can be obtained here, but it must be purified. Also, the spring is very small and use by many people would deplete it. For this short a walk, it's better to carry what you need.

A bit further along the loop, lie the ruins of Van Patten's mountain camp. The ruins of the large buildings are tucked into the base of the canyon wall. Be sure not to climb on the fragile and dangerous ruins. The loop continues back to the same fork. Behind the mountain camp ruins are two oak-shaded picnic tables, ideal resting places on a hot summer day.

HIKE 55 *BAYLOR PASS*

General description: An easy day hike to a pass in the Organ Mountains.
General location: About twenty miles northeast of Las Cruces.
Length: About four miles round trip.
Elevation: 5,680-6,390 feet.
Maps: Organ, Organ Peak NW, and Organ Peak 7.5-minute USGS quads.
Best season: Year round.
Water availability: None.
Special attractions: Views.
Finding the trailhead: Drive about fifteen miles northeast of Interstate 25 in Las Cruces on US 70-82. Just after driving over San Augustin Pass, turn right (south) onto the well-marked Aguirre Springs Recreation Area road. Follow the paved road 5.9 miles to the marked trailhead just before the campground entrance.

The rock needles of the Organ Mountains rise precipitously from the surrounding plains.

The hike: The Organ Mountains are noted for the tall spires that, with their resemblance to organ pipes, give the mountains their name. The mountains rise over 5,000 feet above the Rio Grande Valley to the west. Rock climbers regularly scale the sheer peaks, but without good training and plenty of experience, don't attempt to climb any of the summits. A number of people have died over the years in falls and rockslides.

The trail climbs steadily from the trailhead, trending northwest overall. The trail winds through occasional boulders and rock formations. Scattered oaks and junipers offer shade along the route. As you climb, views to the east and northeast get better and better. To the south tower the igneous crags of the Organ Needles. A particularly good viewpoint is reached shortly before the end of the hike at about 1.5 miles.

Baylor Pass is reached at about two miles. The pass is named after the Confederate general who went through the pass in 1861 to capture Union troops located at San Augustin Springs.

From the pass, the view looks down on Baylor Canyon and a little of the Rio Grande Valley beyond. The west side of the mountains are much more dominated by desert vegetation than the east side. The trail can be easily followed about four miles farther, down Baylor Canyon to the Baylor Canyon Road.

The west trailhead is located about 1.9 miles south of US 70-82 on the Baylor Canyon Road.

The Aguirre Springs Campground at the trailhead is an excellent place to spend the night before or after the hike.

There are tables and pit toilets, but no running water. The hike is good all year, but can be hot in summer. Spring winds can be strong, especially at the pass.

HIKE 56 *PINE TREE TRAIL*

General description: An easy to moderate day hike below the rugged crags of the Organ Needles.
General location: About twenty miles northeast of Las Cruces.
Length: About 4.5 miles round trip.
Elevation: 5,700-6,880 feet.
Maps: BLM brochure, Organ Peak 7.5-minute USGS quad.
Best season: Year round.
Water availability: Usually a reliable stream.
Special attractions: Rugged peaks above trail; views; enormous alligator junipers.
Finding the trailhead: Drive about fifteen miles northeast of Interstate 25 in Las Cruces on US 70-82. Just after driving over San Augustin Pass, turn right (south) onto the well-marked Aguirre Springs Recreation Area road. Follow the paved road 6.1 miles to the marked trailhead just past the campground entrance.

The hike: The Organ Mountains were originally named the Mountains of Solitude by the Spaniards. Later settlers renamed the mountains because of

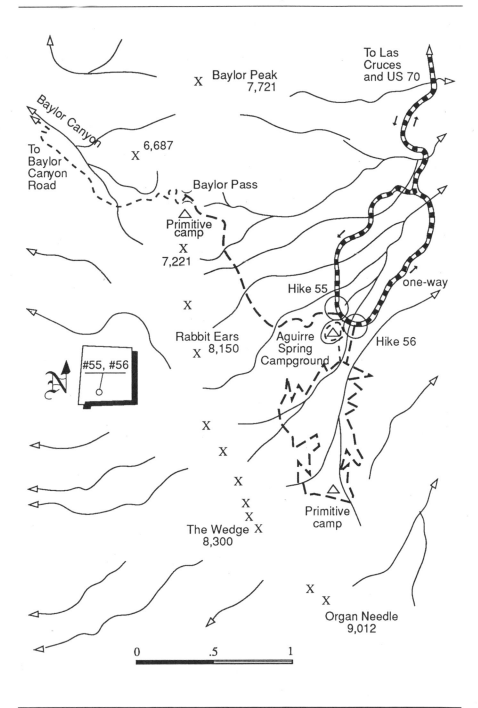

X Baylor Peak
7,721

To Las Cruces and US 70

Baylor Canyon

To Baylor Canyon Road

X 6,687

Baylor Pass

△ Primitive camp

X 7,221

Hike 55

one-way

Rabbit Ears
X 8,150

Aguirre Spring Campground

Hike 56

N #55, #56

X

X

X
X X
The Wedge X
8,300

△ Primitive camp

X X
Organ Needle
9,012

0 .5 1

the resemblance of the rock spires to the pipes in an organ. The sheer spires or needles of the central peaks are made of monzonite uplifted in a fault block and eroded into the present jagged form.

The trail basically follows a broad loop around a drainage basin at the base of Rabbit Ears and several of the other Needles. From the trailhead, the well-constructed trail climbs steadily uphill through scattered oak-juniper woodland. Within less than 0.25 mile, the trail hits the loop. Go right. Within fifty yards a trail forks off to the right and drops back down to another trailhead in the campground. Continue to climb to the left up a steady grade.

The trail winds through boulders tumbled from the heights above and passes by ponderosa pines scattered along the creek bottoms. Some of the largest, most gnarled alligator juniper I have ever seen lie along the trail. Some of the trunks are four or five feet in diameter.

At close to halfway along the loop, the trail traverses around a hillside, reaching a prominent point with tremendous views of the Tularosa Valley, the San Andres Mountains, and even the distant 12,000-foot peak of Sierra Blanca in the Sacramento Mountains. A short climb further and the trail reaches the formal primitive campground, tucked onto a bench wooded with scattered oak, alligator junipers, and ponderosa pine. The primitive camp is one of the few sites along the hike that is level enough to camp on. A few other sites are possible farther down the return leg of the loop.

The camp is located at both the highest point of the hike and about the halfway point. From there, the trail drops steadily down to the end of the loop. About 0.5 mile past the camp, the trail crosses a small stream that is usually reliable, except in very dry spells. Be sure to purify the water. The trail recrosses the same stream just before reaching the end of the loop.

The trail is well-built, but has become heavily eroded in places because of shortcutting. Try to resist the temptation.

The Aguirre Springs Campground at the trailhead is an excellent place to spend the night before or after the hike. There are tables and pit toilets but no running water. The hike is good all year but can be hot in summer. The common spring winds do not affect this hike as much as most areas in southern New Mexico. The towering peaks just to the west of the trail provide shelter from the southwesterly winds. The last time I hiked the trail in spring, I could hear a steady roar as the wind howled through the crags above, but no more than a breeze touched me.

HIKE 57 *WHITE SANDS*

General description: A very easy hike through sand dunes to a back country campsite.

General location: About fifteen miles southwest of Alamogordo.

Length: 0.6 miles round trip.

Elevation: 3,975-4,000 feet.

Maps: Holloman 15-minute USGS quad.

Best season: Year round.

Water availability: none.

Special attractions: The world's largest gypsum dune field.

Permit: Required for camping; obtain at visitor center.

Finding the trailhead: Drive about fifteen miles southwest of Alamogordo on Highway 70 to the entrance of White Sands National Monument. From the visitor center at the entrance, drive into the monument 4.9 miles along the Heart of the Sands Loop Drive to the marked parking lot for the back country campsite.

HIKE 57 *WHITE SANDS*

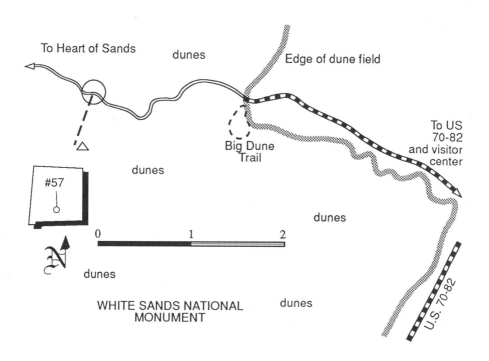

The hike: White Sands lies in the center of a large fault-created basin surrounded by high mountains such as the Sacramentos, Organs, San Andres, and Oscura Mountains. For millenia, rain and melting snow have carried dissolved gypsum down into the basin from large deposits in these mountains. The gypsum is carried to Lake Lucero, the lowest point in the basin. The hot desert sun dries the lake waters, leaving a lake bed covered with gypsum crystals. The prevailing southwest wind erodes the crystals into fine grains and sweeps them away to the northeast in endless ranks of dunes.

This hike is exceptionally easy hike, included because of the uniqueness of White Sands. From the parking area, follow a series of numbered marker posts southwest 0.3 mile to the campsite, marked with a large sign. Markers are used because the wind can obliterate all tracks within hours. The trail climbs over several dunes, but otherwise the route is level and very short. The camping area is in a flat area between the dunes.

Be sure to camp if you have time. On a night with a full moon, the almost snow-white dunes are very bright. Be sure not to take anything that you don't want to get sandy. Since the monument doesn't open until after sunrise, camping is the only way to see the dunes at sunrise.

Don't let the shortness of the trail prevent you from exploring further. Take day hikes farther out into the dunes and enjoy the endless expanse of sand. Occasional cottonwoods, with many of their roots exposed, break up the sameness of the terrain. Yucca, rabbitbrush, four-wing saltbush, and other shrubs manage a tenuous hold on life in the shifting sands. Be sure to take the Big Dune Trail, a nature trail, two miles from the visitor center along the Loop Drive, to learn more about the dunes.

Be extremely careful when leaving the established roads or trails. Use a compass, maps, and landmarks to avoid becoming lost. Spring is the most likely time for wind and sandstorms.

Wear dark glasses and sunscreen, because the sand is extremely bright. At times the dunes are closed to overnight camping because of military testing at adjacent White Sands Missile Range. You may want to call ahead to determine if any testing is planned.

The largest gypsum dune field in the world lies at White Sands National Monument.

HIKE 58 *CAPITAN PEAK*

General description: A strenuous two or three day backpack into one of the least visited wildernesses in New Mexico.

General location: About fifty miles west of Roswell.

Length: About twenty miles round trip.

Elevation: 6,300-10,083 feet.

Maps: Lincoln National Forest, Arroyo Serrano West, Arabela, Kyle Harrison Canyon, and Capitan Peak 7.5-minute USGS quads.

Best season: Late April through mid-November.

Water availability: Seasonal in Pine Lodge, Copeland, and Seven Cabins Canyons; see text.

Special attractions: Lush old growth conifer forest; views of much of the state; solitude.

Finding the trailhead: Drive four miles north of the center of Roswell on US Highway 285 to the junction with NM 246. Turn left and drive west about fifty miles to the junction with the dirt FR 130 (the sign says Boy Scout Mountain). Or from Capitan, follow 246 about thirty-two miles north and east to the junction. Follow FR 130 southeast about 3.9 miles to the large North Base Trail 65 sign and park. With care, the rocky FR 130 can usually be negotiated with passenger cars; however, it would be best to call the Lincoln National Forest ranger station in Capitan first for current road conditions.

The hike: The Capitan Mountains are one of the few ranges in the United States that run east-west. The steep rugged mountains, rising abruptly from the high plains of southeastern New Mexico, are the first mountains seen by visitors entering New Mexico from the much of the eastern part of the state. On clear days, the Capitans can be seen from as far away as the Texas state line.

In 1950, a 17,000-acre forest fire raged for several days in the western end of the mountains. A small burned black bear cub was found clinging to a charred tree. After receiving veterinary care, he was flown to the National Zoo in Washington, D.C. to become the national symbol of forest fire prevention, Smokey Bear.

The steep, higher elevations of the eastern end of the Capitans were too difficult to enter with logging roads, so they have never been timbered. In recent years, much of the east section has been designated the Capitan Mountain Wilderness. Dense old growth forests of Douglas fir and spruce greet hikers willing to make the strenuous climb up into the Capitans.

Even though the popular resort towns of Ruidoso and Cloudcroft are not far to the south, the Capitans are almost completely undiscovered. Except during hunting season, you may well hike the entire twenty-mile loop without seeing another person.

The creeks in Pine Lodge, Copeland, and Seven Cabins Canyons run much of the year, often even year round. Inquire at the Capitan ranger office for their current status. On this hike, Seven Cabins Creek is most useful, because it allows hikers to avoid carrying much water for the first five miles of the loop. The other two canyons are too close to the trailhead to be of much use. There is no reliable water on the mountain crest, so either carry sufficient water or load up at Seven Cabins Creek. Purify if you use the stream water.

The first section of the route, Trail 65, contours west along the base of the mountains, crossing numerous drainages.

Almost the entire hike is in heavy forest. The only part of the hike that can be confusing is the first five miles along the North Base Trail because of a network of old logging roads.

The route at the trailhead starts initially as an old dirt road. It immediately drops down into and crosses Pine Lodge Creek. On the other side, the bank is covered with fire rings from hunter camps. Look for the Trail 65 sign at the west side of the area of hunters'campsites (only 100 yards or so from the creek). The trail trends west through a mixed alligator juniper, pinyon, oak, and ponderosa pine forest. A little more than a mile from the start, you hit a T-shaped junction with a Trail 65 sign. Take the left fork of the "T" uphill. You are now on a faint old road again. A few hundred yards further, a faint trail goes uphill to the left. Ignore it and stay on the more travelled righthand route. Ignore another faint lefthand trail another one-half mile further and drop down into a creek bottom on the more-travelled trail instead. After crossing the dry creek and climbing out, you reach an old road junction. Take the righthand fork, marked by a Trail 65 sign, even though in this case it appears to be the less-travelled route. Trail 65 and the rest of the route are well-marked by tree blazes. Within a half-mile of the junction, the old road ends and reverts to a trail in the bottom of a dry creek.

A trailside sign denotes Red Lick Canyon at about three miles. At 3.5 miles the trail hits F.R. 163 coming up Copeland Canyon. At the junction, signs indicate the proper route, up the road to the left (south) for about one-quarter mile. A trail sign marks the turnoff to the right (west again). In about 100 yards the trail crosses the small stream of Copeland Creek, marked with a sign. The trail is faint for a bit just after crossing the creek. It turns downstream and parallels the creek for a short distance before climbing the bank and continuing west again.

At five miles, the trail crosses the stream at Seven Cabins Canyon and hits a thicket of trail junction signs. Just downhill to the right is the end of FR 256, but turn left (south) up the canyon on Trail 66. You enter the Capitan Mountain Wilderness within fifty yards. Although the trail is in excellent condition, Trail 66 is the toughest part of the loop because of the 2,300-foot gain in the four miles to the crest at Pierce Canyon Pass. The first part of the climb follows the canyon bottom, passing groves of bigtooth maples, beautiful in October. If you need water, be sure to get it here before the trail starts switchbacking up out of the canyon bottom.

Several flat ridge-top areas make decent campsites along the climb, but if you have enough energy, the crest is the best area for camping with numerous level needle-carpeted sites in the old growth timber.

At the four-way marked intersection on the crest, turn left (east) on Trail 58, the Summit Trail. The area around the intersection would make a good first night's campsite. The sign indicates a distance of three miles to Capitan Peak, but it appears to be more like 3.5 miles. The difficult part of the hike is over. The Summit Trail climbs very gradually east toward the summit of Capitan Peak through lush virgin stands of Douglas fir, spruce, and aspen.

At about 12.5 miles the trail climbs into the lower end of a clearing with a sign saying "Capitan Peak, 10,083 feet." A short side trail leads to a Forest Service cabin, visible above in the trees. Please don't disturb it or any of the fire equipment and other gear stored in it. Be sure to take the time to climb

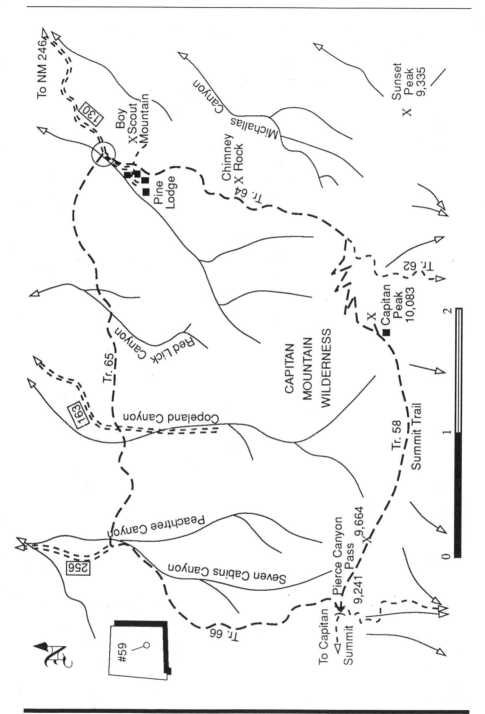

up through the clearing above the sign the few hundred yards to the bare summit of Capitan Peak. On clear days, 360-degree views reveal mountains as distant as the Sangre de Cristos above Santa Fe and the Guadalupe Mountains of West Texas. Level areas in the trees just below the peak would make an excellent site for a second night's camp. Watching the sunrise or sunset from the summit is hard to beat.

The descent back to the trailhead is long, dropping almost 4,000 feet in about seven miles, so take your time and enjoy the almost continuous views. After leaving Capitan Peak, continue east on Trail 58 as it descends about 1.5 miles to the junction of Trails 62 and 64. Along the way you'll pass another faint route climbing off to the right to the summit of Capitan Peak. At the junction, turn left on Trail 64 to FR 130. The trail descends through many switchbacks; please don't shortcut. Right after leaving the wilderness near the end of the hike, you'll pass by the first cabin of Pine Lodge.

After passing above several more cabins, the trail intersects another trail in the bottom of a dry creek. Ignore it; its left fork goes to the cabins and the right fork climbs up the dry creek. Trail 64 soon hits FR 130 only about 100 yards up from the starting point at the North Base Trailhead.

Trail 64 can be climbed by itself to Capitan Peak as a strenuous day hike. An easier day hike or overnight trip would be to drive to the end of FR 256 in Seven Cabins Canyon and hike up Trail 66 to Pierce Canyon Pass. To avoid the steep climb up to the crest altogether, drive up the very rough FR 56 from Capitan Pass to the start of the Summit Trail at Capitan Summit.

HIKE 59 *TUCSON MOUNTAIN*

General description: A moderate day hike or easy overnight trip to the top of a subrange of the Sacramento Mountains.
General location: About forty miles north of Ruidoso.
Length: About ten miles round trip.
Elevation: 6,880-8,333 feet.
Maps: Lincoln National Forest, White Oaks South 7.5-minute USGS quad.
Best season: April through November.
Water availability: Goat Spring.
Special attractions: Open, park-like stands of ponderosa pine; views.
Finding the trailhead: Drive twelve miles west of Capitan on US 380. Across from the junction with NM 37, turn right (north) onto the excellent gravel Forest Road 441. Ignore the incredible array of "No Tresspassing" signs along 441; the public has right of way access to the forest boundary. Just past the impressive O-Bar-O Ranch headquarters, you will reach the Forest Service boundary at about 5.5 miles. After passing through the boundary gate (leave it as you find it), the road gets steeper and rougher. Depending on road conditions, sometimes a passenger car can make it to the trailhead. However, a high clearance vehicle is recommended.

The well-marked Tucson Mountain trailhead is only a mile up the road from the Forest Service boundary, so park and walk the extra distance if in doubt about the road. The large sign marking the trailhead is on the right side as the road enters a large grassy meadow.

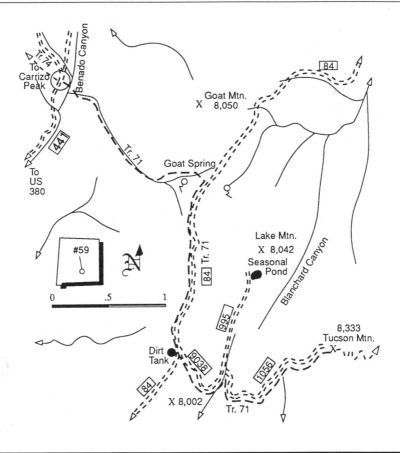

The hike: Tucson Mountain is the highest point in the Vera Cruz Mountains, a small subrange of the Sacramento Mountains.

It connects with the larger Capitan Mountains to the east by a 7,000-foot pass traversed by NM 246 and connects to the west with the Carrizo Mountains by another low pass crossed by FR 441. The trail climbs gradually from pinyon-juniper forest into pure stands of ponderosa on the broad summit. The trail is easy to follow, but since several of the junctions aren't marked, be sure to follow the directions carefully.

From the trailhead sign, Trail 71 isn't obvious. Look east fifty yards away or so for a blaze on a ponderosa. From the blazed ponderosa, cross the tiny dry creek behind it and then drop into the main dry creek bottom. You should be on a faint old road that ends in the creek a few yards from where you stand. The trail is quite obvious as it crosses the creek to the southeast as an extension of the old road. Shortly after climbing out of the main creek, it drops back down into a southeast-trending dry tributary. The trail follows the creek all the way to Goat Spring at about 1.5 miles. It crosses back and forth from bank to bank. The creek bottom is densely wooded with ponderosa, oak, Douglas fir, and alligator juniper and offers many good campsites. Don't expect to see anyone on this hike, especially the section leading to Goat Spring. Be careful in deer season, however, as the trail does see significant use then.

At about 1.5 miles, water from Goat Spring appears, trickling down the canyon bottom. The trail climbs high up the left (north) bank for a few hundred yards when you reach the water. It rejoins the creek at the small pool at Goat Spring, marked with a sign. If you get water, be sure to purify it.

About one-quarter mile beyond the spring, the trail hits a dirt road, little-used FR 84. Turn right (south) on the road and follow it about 1.5 miles to the junction with FR 9038 at a dirt cattle tank. As you climb, you pass grassy meadows with scattered park-like stands of ponderosa. Turn left at the tank and follow FR 9038 up the hill for about one-half mile to the junction where FR 9038 splits into FR 1056 and FR 995. The junction occurs in a large meadow.

From FR 9038 onwards, the camping opportunities become more and more inviting. Turn right onto the much fainter fork, FR 1056. From here, wind up the old road through open meadows and stands of ponderosa to the broad wooded summit of the mountain. About a mile past the 1056/995 junction, you'll pass a yellow stone aerial marker in a meadow. The summit is a short distance beyond. An old well of some sort, a large rock cairn, and the foundation of what looks to be an old fire lookout crown the summit. From the crest, the best views are to the east and southeast of Capitan and the Capitan Mountains. Move down the crest of the summit to the west a bit for good views of the Carrizo, Patos, and Jicarilla mountains. Return the same way.

Trail 71 continues on down the east side of Tucson Mountain to FR 165. A more difficult, but spectacular, trail is Trail 74 up Johnnie Canyon to the much higher (9656 feet) Carrizo Peak. Its marked trailhead is just across FR 441 from the Tucson Mountain trailhead.

HIKE 60 *SIERRA BLANCA*

General description: A strenuous day hike to the summit of the highest mountain in southern New Mexico.
General location: About 20 miles northwest of Ruidoso.
Length: About 9.25 miles round trip.
Elevation: 9,830-11,973 feet.
Maps: White Mountain Wilderness, Lincoln National Forest, Sierra Blanca 15-minute USGS quad.
Best season: May through October.
Water availability: Ice Spring usually reliable.
Special attractions: Tremendous views, alpine tundra.
Permit: Since the summit lies within the Mescalero Apache Reservation, inquire at tribal headquarters in Mescalero whether permission is necessary.
Finding the trailhead: Take NM 48 about seven miles north of Ruidoso to the well-marked junction with NM 532. Turn left (west) and follow it twelve miles all the way up to the end of the road at the ski area. The windy and steep, but paved, road is one of the most spectacular in the state. The trailhead is at the small parking area on the last highway curve just before you enter the main ski area parking lot.

The hike: The USGS designates the entire mountain range from the Jicarillas in the north to just north of north end of the Guadalupes in the south as the Sacramento Mountains. The names of distinct subranges are used for more specific identification. The large part of the range south of Highway 70, centered around Cloudcroft, is generally known as the Sacramentos. Other subranges include the Capitans, Jicarillas, Patos, Sierra Blanca, Carrizo, and Vera Cruz mountains. Although passes and divides separate the subranges and many were formed from different geological processes, the entire range is high enough to be continuously forested.

The Sierra Blanca Range reaches the highest point, not only in the Sacramentos, but in the entire state except for the Sangre de Cristo Mountains in the north. The huge extrusive volcanic mountain at Sierra Blanca Peak towers 7,800 feet above the Tularosa Valley for the greatest relief in New Mexico. The peak and surrounding ridges and summits are the only area in southern New Mexico to rise above timberline into alpine tundra vegetation. Small moraines and cirques indicate that the peak was probably glaciated in the Pleistocene. The climb to the summit is popular in summer; try to avoid weekends if possible.

Take marked Trail 15 from the parking lot up along a small creek and then up a grassy hillside about 0.6 mile (although the sign says 0.5 mile) to the junction with Crest Trail 25. Go left (west) on Trail 25 toward the Lookout Mountain Trail, about two miles away. The trail traverses a heavily wooded hillside across from the ski area. Some of the Douglas firs in the old growth forest are as large as five feet in diameter. At a little more than one-half mile beyond the junction, the trail enters a grassy sloping valley with many good campsites possible. Faded orange-painted fence posts mark the trail across the small valley. The trail switchbacks up into dense spruce and fir on a north

A late spring snow dusts 12,000-foot Sierra Blanca, the highest peak in southern New Mexico.

slope, leaving the ski area behind for a time. This section of trail can have snow well into early summer; check with the Forest Service in Ruidoso before starting early season hikes.

The trail curves back around into sight of the ski area and climbs steadily to the junction with Lookout Mountain Trail 78, about 2.6 miles from the trailhead. Ice Spring lies in the draw just below the junction. Turn left (south) onto Trail 78 and climb steadily to the crest of the range. After you reach the crest, you climb above timberline, so, if you are camping, you may want to pick a site before then.

The trail climbs steadily, passing the buildings at the top of the ski area gondola before reaching the summit of Lookout Mountain at 11,580 feet and about 0.8 mile from the Trail 78 junction. The formal trail ends at Lookout Mountain, but Sierra Blanca Peak looms about 1.25 miles south. A well-worn route follows the crest down across a divide and back up the last steep climb to the summit. The tundra, covered with flowers in summer, is very fragile, so try to stay on the worn route rather than trampling other areas. The summit gives some of the best views in the state, from the Guadalupe Mountains of West Texas to the Sangre de Cristos above Santa Fe to the Gila Wilderness far to the west. If desired, your return route can follow some of the ski runs back down the mountain, although they can be steep.

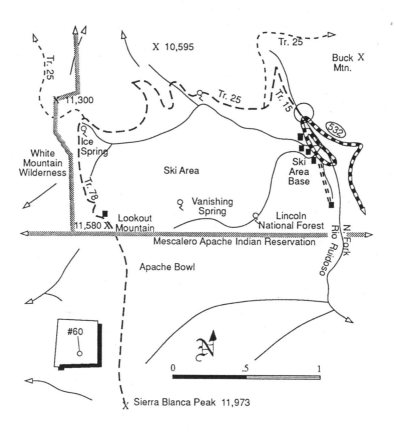

X 10,595

Tr. 25

Buck X
Mtn.

Tr. 25

Tr. 25

Tr. 15

532

11,300

Ice
Spring

White
Mountain
Wilderness

Tr. 78

Ski Area

Ski
Area
Base

Vanishing
Spring

Lookout
Mountain

11,580 X

Lincoln
National Forest

N. Fork Rio Ruidoso

Mescalero Apache Indian Reservation

Apache Bowl

#60

N

0   .5   1

X Sierra Blanca Peak 11,973

Even though the hike is in southern New Mexico, the area above timberline can be very cold and windy even in summer. Take adequate clothes on the hike. Try to start the hike early in the morning, since summer thunderstorms build extremely quickly on the peak, especially in the afternoon. Ideally, you should be starting down the mountain after lunch time. The area above timberline is not a good place to be caught in a lightning storm.

HIKE 61 *MONJEAU LOOKOUT*

General description: A moderate dayhike or easy overnight trip (an easy day hike with a car shuttle) along a high ridge of the White Mountain Wilderness.
General location: About twenty miles northwest of Ruidoso.
Length: About 11.25 miles round trip.
Elevation: 9,120-10,460 feet.
Maps: White Mountain Wilderness, Lincoln National Forest, Sierra Blanca 15-minute and Angus 7.5-minute USGS quads.
Best season: May through October, depending on snow.
Water availability: none.
Special attractions: Aspens in fall, excellent views of the White Mountain Wilderness.
Finding the trailhead: This hike shares the same trailhead as Hike 60, Sierra Blanca; see the directions there.

The hike: This hike follows a section of the Crest Trail from the ski area along a long scenic ridge to the access road just below the fire lookout on Monjeau Peak. The enormous stands of aspen along the hike turn the hillsides gold in October.

The trail starts at about 9,830 feet and climbs within the first two miles to the high point at about 10,460 feet. For the most part, the rest of the hike is a slow easy descent along the ridge to a low point of about 9,120 feet. The last 0.25 mile climbs about 200 feet up to the lookout access road, FR 117.

From the parking area, take marked Trail 15 up a creek and across a grassy hillside about 0.6 mile (although the sign says 0.5 mile) to the junction with Crest Trail 25. Turn right (north) onto Trail 25 (Hike 60 turns left here). In a few hundred yards the trail reenters the forest in a stand of enormous virgin spruce. It soon returns to an open grassy area and begins climbing. At the upper end of the meadow, about 0.5 mile from the Trail 15 junction, the trail forks at a junction marked only by an old fence post. Take the right (east fork), rather than switchbacking up the hill to the left. In about fifty yards the trail hits the dirt road leading up to the radio towers on Buck Mountain. Follow the road to the right (southeast) for about fifty yards, where the trail leaves the road by climbing uphill to the left. In about 100 yards, the trail hits the road again. Follow the road to the right (southeast) again for about 100 yards until the trail again forks uphill to the left, away from the road. In effect, the trail simply cuts across a large switchback in the road.

The other fork at the unmarked trail junction just below the road also climbs up to the road, joining it at a different spot.

Within about 200 yards of the road, the trail reaches its high point on a forested hill and then begins the long slow descent along the ridge top to Monjeau Lookout. About one-half mile from the high point, the trail reaches a large bare windswept section of ridge with a chewed-up White Mountain Wilderness boundary sign. The views are tremendous, from Nogal Peak across the Rio Bonito drainage to the distant Manzano Mountains far to the northwest.

The rest of the route is visible to the east, as it follows the alternately wooded and bare ridge all the way to the lookout. Campsites abound along the ridgetop,

Aspens are common in the White Mountain Wilderness.

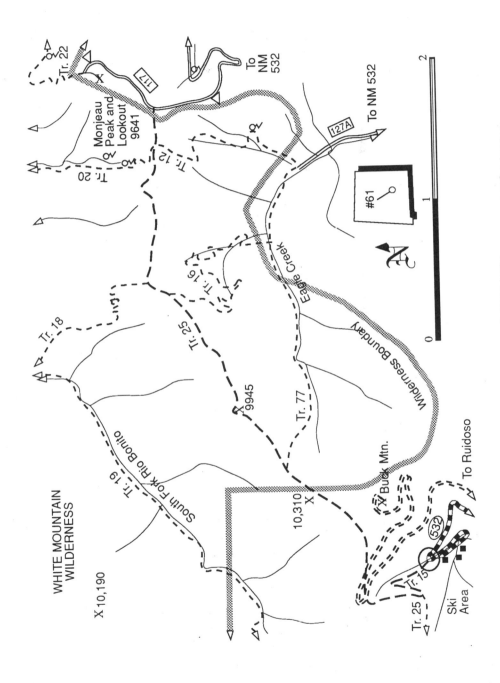

although there are no easily accessible springs, unlike much of the rest of the Crest Trail. Since the trail does follow the ridgetop for the most part, be careful about lightning storms.

Junctions for trails 77, 16, 18, 12, and 20 will be passed, but just stay on Trail 25 along the the ridgetop. At about 5.5 miles, the trail hits FR 117 after a short climb. If you have set up a car shuttle, your hike is over, otherwise return the same way. If you have time, be sure to walk up to the lookout, less than a mile and only a few hundred feet above you. Its 360-degree views are hard to beat.

HIKE 62 ARGENTINA CANYON

General description: A moderately easy hike through the high forest of the White Mountain Wilderness.
General location: About twenty-five miles northwest of Ruidoso.
Length: About 6.5 miles round trip.
Elevation: 7,800-9,100 feet.
Maps: White Mountain Wilderness, Lincoln National Forest, Sierra Blanca Peak 15-minute USGS quad.
Best season: May to mid-November.
Water availability: Argentina Spring, Spring Cabin Spring.
Special attractions: Lush virgin forest with running streams, tremendous views.
Finding the trailhead: Drive ten miles south of Capitan on NM 48 and turn right (west) onto NM 37 or drive about twelve miles north of Ruidoso on NM 48 and turn left (west) onto NM 37. Follow 37 about 1.3 miles to the paved and marked Bonito Lake and South Fork Campground turnoff on the left (FR 107). Follow FR 107 about nine miles to the end of the road, passing Bonito Lake on the way. The road turns to gravel after the South Fork Campground turnoff. The trail starts from the large parking lot at the end of the road.

The hike: The White Mountain Wilderness is a 49,000-acre tract ranging from 6,000 to 11,500 feet in elevation. For the most part, its boundaries contain the high crest that encircles the Rio Bonito drainage. The wilderness and adjacent Sierra Blanca Peak are the highest mountains in southern New Mexico and have alpine tundra and glaciation scars from recent ice ages. The mountains' height and abrupt rise (7,800 feet of relief) from the Tularosa Valley to the west allow the mountains to trap considerable rain and snow.

Thus, the mountains are blessed with many permanent springs and streams. Unlike many New Mexico mountains, quite a few springs occur along the crest of the range, limiting the need for backpackers to carry large amounts of water. This hike follows one of many possible loops along running streams to the crest of the range. The wilderness is a popular area with many hikers, especially on summer weekends.

Follow the signs on the north side of the parking lot to Argentina Canyon Trail 39. The trail climbs steadily up the canyon along a running stream for 2.5 miles to the Crest Trail, passing enormous Douglas fir trees. In a grassy

Idyllic campsites are easy to find in the White Mountain Wilderness.

meadow at about 1.75 miles, a marked trail, Cut Across Trail 38, forks to the left. Should you desire to shorten the hike, you can follow Trail 38 to the Little Bonito Trail 37 and cut off the upper part of the loop. However, if possible, stay with Trail 39 so that you won't miss the tremendous views along the Crest Trail. The trail passes through a large aspen grove at the head of the canyon, beautiful in fall. A short rocky stretch brings you to marked Argentina Spring at the edge of the broad treeless crest. Get water, if necessary, from the plastic pipe at the spring. Purify it. Trail 39 joins Crest Trail 25 about 100 yards west across the grassy meadow. Trail 42 joins 39 from the east at Argentina Spring. Stay with 39 to the Crest Trail. The best camping in this area is probably back down trail 39 a short distance in the aspen grove.

Turn left (south) on the Crest Trail and follow it for 1.25 miles to the next trail junction. Much of the first part of the Crest Trail is bare, giving tremendous views of the the Rio Bonito drainage to the east. To the north and west, the mountains drop off sharply into the Tularosa Valley. Across the valley, with its black Malpais lava flow, lies the Sierra Oscura. Multitudes of other mountain ranges are visible on clear days.

At a grassy saddle the trail hits a well-marked five-way junction. The Crest Trail continues south and makes up two of the trails. The Doherty Ridge Trail 50 goes right and drops down into the Tularosa Valley to the west. The trail that you want, 37, angles sharply left (northeast). The well-worn fifth trail is

HIKE 62 *ARGENTINA CANYON*

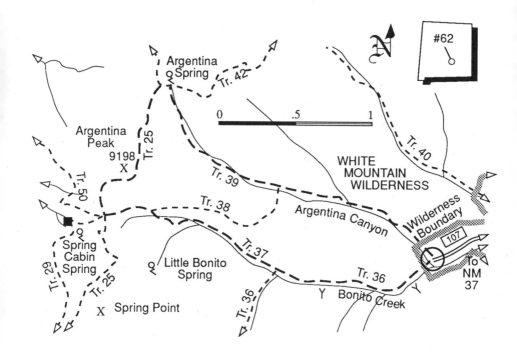

the only unmarked trail. If you need water or want a good campsite, follow it southwest of the junction onto the north side of a slight ridge. In about a .25 mile, passing good campsites as you go, the trail reaches Spring Cabin, a Forest Service cabin. Don't camp right by the cabin.

If you need water, follow an unmarked trail trending southeast from the cabin for about two hundred yards to Spring Cabin Spring in a draw.

From the five-way junction, Trail 37 descends steeply along flowing Little Bonito Creek for about 1.25 miles to the junction with Bonito Creek. About one-quarter mile down 37, you will pass Trail 38, the Cut Across Trail, on your left.

At the junction with Bonito Creek and Bonito Trail 36, turn left on Trail 36. An easy 1.25-mile walk down Trail 36 along a rushing stream past two old mines brings you back to the trailhead.

The loop can be enlarged considerably by following the Crest Trail farther south from the five-way junction to Trail 36 and following it all the way down Bonito Creek and back to the trailhead. Another considerably longer and more strenuous loop is possible from the South Fork Campground trailhead.

Follow Trail 19 to the crest and return via Trail 33. Many other loops are possible; all are beautiful with running streams and great views. A loop involving the entire crest trail would be on the order of twenty-five miles long.

HIKE 63 *SACRAMENTO RIM*

General description: An easy two or three day backpack following the high western rim of the Sacramento Mountains.
General location: About two miles south of the center of Cloudcroft.
Length: Twenty-eight miles round trip (fourteen miles with car shuttle), multiple trailheads allow the hike to be shortened or lengthened as desired.
Elevation: 8,360-9,500 feet.
Maps: Lincoln National Forest, Sacramento Peak and High Rolls 7.5-minute USGS quads.
Best season: May through November, depending on snow.
Water availability: none.
Special attractions: Lush mountain forest, views.
Finding the trailhead: From the center of Cloudcroft, drive 1.9 miles south on Highway 130 to the junction with the paved highway leading to Sunspot and Timberon. Turn right on it and go about 0.1 miles to Slide Group Campground. Park in the gravel area along the highway at the campground entrance.

The hike: The mountain range around Cloudcroft has the same name as the entire series of ranges that stretches from the Jicarilla Mountains far north of Ruidoso to a point far south of Cloudcroft. The subrange known as the Sacramento Mountains is the largest, although not highest, range and runs south from Tularosa Canyon, traversed by Highway 70, to near the Guadalupe Mountains at Pinon. The mountains formed as a huge fault block lifted up sharply from the floor of the Tularosa Valley. On the west, the mountains rise abruptly in two steps, with deep rugged canyons and towering cliffs of Permian and Pennsylvanian limestones. To the east, the mountains slope gradually downwards from lush fir and aspen forest to the desert scrub of the Pecos River Valley.

The crest or rim of the rugged west side lies above 9,000 feet for over twenty miles. The Rim Trail, 105, follows the rim for many miles south of Cloudcroft. It was the first National Forest Trail in New Mexico to be designated a National Recreation Trail. The trail has some ups and downs as it crosses drainages, but in general it is a very easy, but long, trail. No good water sources exist along the route, but water caches can be easily set up in advance because of the trail's multiple access points. The trail generally parallels the highway to Sunspot, but usually lies a considerable distance to the west. Although I've never encountered motorcycles, they are permitted on the Rim Trail. Probably summer weekends are the most likely time for such activity.

Large signs mark the start of the popular hike at the entrance to the campground. Go left at the large Rim Trail sign, not down the gully to the right into Deer Head Campground. The trail quickly passes Slide Campground, staying not far from the highway for most of the first mile.

Just before the one-mile point, the trail touches the Sunspot highway again, forming an alternate trailhead. After this secondary trailhead, the trail turns sharply west leaving the highway behind. The well-developed trail has mile markers for the entire fourteen miles (although some have been vandalized), making it easy to determine your location.

171

After the one-mile marker, the trail continues out onto the end of a long ridge, giving some of the best views of the entire hike. The Tularosa Valley stretches for miles 5,000 feet below, with the snow white dunes of White Sands easily visible. To the north, frequently snow-capped 12,000-foot Sierra Blanca towers into the sky. The trail quickly doubles back into the lush Douglas fir, spruce, and aspen forest of the rim. At about 2.25 miles, the trail crosses the old road going down grassy Haynes Canyon. Between miles two and three, the trail passes through extensive groves of bigtooth maples, known for their brilliant gold and scarlet fall color. In October, this stretch of trail can be eight inches deep in maple, oak, and aspen leaves.

Just past mile three, the trail crosses another small canyon with a faint trail going up and down it. The grassy canyon makes an excellent camping area. At about 4.5 miles, the trail crosses well-marked FR 636. The trail joins FR 636 at about 5.5 miles only about fifty yards before it joins the Sunspot Highway. Follow 636 up to the highway intersection.

The trail continues on by dropping down below the highway to the right (south) in front of the stop sign. This is another good, easily found trailhead.

At about 6.75 miles the trail hits a junction in a small open grassy canyon bottom. Trail 105 is marked as going uphill to the left, but it only goes a short distance up to another marked trailhead on the Sunspot Highway, across from Russia Canyon. Unless you're ending your hike here, continue straight ahead on the Rim Trail, also 105.

At about 7.25 miles, a faint trail joins the main trail from a large meadow on the left, a beautiful camping area. After about the eight mile point, excellent level campsites become more and more common. At almost nine miles the trail crosses a well-maintained logging road. The trail crosses Karr Canyon Road (FR 63) at about 10.25 miles. The junction is well-marked and makes another good trailhead. If necessary, water can be obtained by walking down Karr Canyon to a series of travertine springs. Just before the eleven-mile point, the trail crosses the paved Alamo Peak road, another possible trailhead.

Just after the Alamo Peak road, the trail crosses a combined powerline and logging road. At about 11.25 miles a side trail branches off to the left. Ignore it. The trail crosses an unused old logging road just short of twelve miles. At about 13.75 miles the trail reaches a huge grassy meadow, Atkinson Field. The trail circles the meadow, remaining in the forest, and crosses FR 640 at about fourteen miles, the end of this hike.

By going left, FR 640 leads back to the Sunspot Highway in about 1.4 miles. Trail 105 can be followed further, if desired.

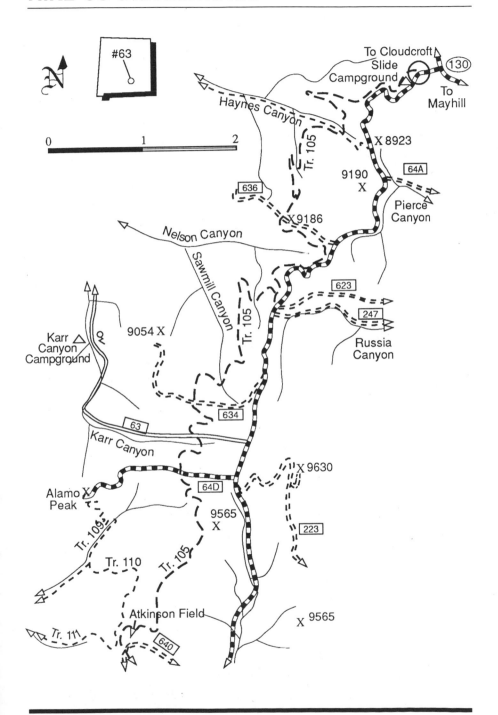

HIKE 64 *BLUFF SPRINGS*

General description: An easy day hike along abandoned grades of the historic Cloudcroft logging railroad.
General location: About fifteen miles south of Cloudcroft.
Length: About five miles round trip.
Elevation: 8,070-8,950 feet.
Maps: Lincoln National Forest, Bluff Springs and Sacramento Peak 7.5-minute USGS quads .
Best season: Mid-April through November.
Water availability: Bluff Springs, small spring at about 1.5 miles.
Special attractions: Waterfall, historic railroad grade, lush forest.
Finding the trailhead: Go about 1.9 miles south of Cloudcroft on Highway 130 to the junction with the Sunspot and Timberon highway. Turn right and follow the Sunspot highway for about nine miles to the Bluff Springs turnoff on the left, combined FR 164 and County Road C17. Follow 164 down the Rio Penasco 3.9 miles to the marked parking area at Bluff Springs. FR 164 is paved for two miles, then turns to gravel at the junction with the Water Canyon road on the right.

The hike: A railroad was built up into the Sacramento Mountains from the Tularosa Valley in 1898 to haul out timber from the heavily forested mountains. Excursion trains were quickly begun by people seeking to escape the summer heat, leading to the opening of the resort area at Cloudcroft in 1899. The railroad was abandoned in 1947, leaving wooden trestles and railroad grades scattered across the higher parts of the mountains south of Cloudcroft. One enormous trestle still stands just west of Cloudcroft along US 82. Rotting ties and rusted railroad spikes evoke images of steam engines chugging slowly through the forest, pulling flat cars loaded with logs. The abandoned grades today make excellent trails for both hiking in summer and cross-country skiing in winter. Unfortunately, motorcycles are allowed on some of the grades.

From the parking lot, cross the foot bridge over the Rio Penasco to the railroad grade on the south river bank. The waterfall above you has formed impressive travertine deposits from calcium carbonate dissolved in the water. The main trail climbs the bluff to the top of the waterfall and the spring's source about a quarter mile away. Be sure to take time to climb up the trail. Obtain and purify water here if you need it. The area around the waterfall is very popular on summer weekends.

The hike, however, turns left at the base of the falls and follows the railroad grade up hill to the east. A large sign indicates the start of the hike up Trail 112, the Willie White Trail Spur. The railroad grade, Trail 112, passes several springs within a few hundred feet of the start. At about 0.25 mile, the trail passes a small wooden railroad trestle. The railroad grade meets Trail 113 climbing up from the left at about 0.5 mile from the start.

Stay on the railroad grade, now Trail 113. The trail gradually climbs up a wooded hillside until it merges with a grassy canyon bottom at about 1.5 miles. An unmarked, lightly used trail goes down the canyon and back to FR 164. Trail 113 continues up the canyon and leaves the railroad grade.

You, however, should turn sharply back left (east) onto marked Trail 9277, the continuation of the railroad grade.

About 300 yards up Trail 9277, you pass a small spring bubbling up beside the railroad grade. The spring is small, but appears to be reliable. About 0.5 mile up from the 9277/113 junction, an unused and overgrown railroad grade forks sharply back to the right (west). Explore it, if you wish, and leave the people behind. A little less than a mile up Trail 9277 from the trail junction, the trail turns sharply back right (west) onto another railroad grade.

Instead, continue east on the same railroad grade for about 0.25 mile to its end. A very faint old road leads up the hill to the right from the end of the railroad grade. You reach the top of the ridge in a hundred yards or so, with level pine needle-covered potential campsites all around. Be very careful once you leave the railroad grades. With no clear landmarks, it's easy to get lost in the dense forest.

Many hikes are possible along the railroad grades. Many spurs lead off of the main lines to old logging camp sites. Trail 9277 can be followed considerably farther. Trail 113 can be followed up over the mountain to the Water Canyon road (FR5009) and back down FR 164 for an easy 7.2-mile loop.

HIKE 64 *BLUFF SPRINGS*

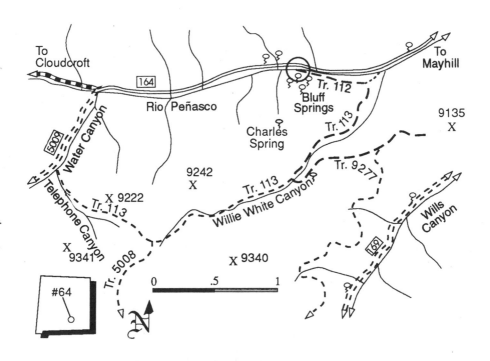

HIKE 65 *DOG CANYON*

General description: A strenuous day hike from the Tularosa Valley up into the Sacramento Mountains.

General location: About fifteen miles south of Alamogordo.

Length: About 8.4 miles round trip.

Elevation: 4,400-7,550 feet.

Maps: Lincoln National Forest, Sacramento Peak and Alamogordo South 7.5-minute USGS quads, Dog Canyon Trail leaflet (National Forest Service).

Best season: Year round.

Water availability: Dog Canyon stream at 2.4 miles.

Special attractions: Desert stream; rugged canyon; views.

Finding the trailhead: Drive about ten miles south of Alamogordo on Highway 54. Turn left (east) on the marked road to Oliver Lee Memorial State Park and drive about four miles to the park visitor center.

The hike: Dog Canyon is one of several canyons in the steep western escarpment of the Sacramento Mountains. The rugged west face of the mountains rises over 5,000 feet within a few miles from the Chihuahuan Desert of the Tularosa Valley to the lush Canadian Zone forest of the crest. The Dog Canyon Trail climbs over 3,100 feet in only 4.2 miles, making it a fairly difficult hike, especially in summer.

Because of the reliable spring-fed stream in the canyon, the trail has been used for thousands of years as a route from the Tularosa Valley into the Sacramento Mountains. After arrival of the white man, the trail was used as a route of retreat by Apaches fleeing military forces. Many battles were fought in the canyon between Apaches and troops from 1850 to 1881. In 1880, sixty soldiers pursued old Chief Nana and his warriors into the canyon. When the troops were on the "Eyebrow," the steep upper portion of the trail, the Indians rolled rocks onto them, killing and injuring many.

The marked trail (106) starts at the foot of the mountains near the visitor center in the state park. Camping with showers is available in the park. The first 0.4 mile is a steep climb up the mountain slope. The hillside is very susceptible to erosion; try to resist the urge to shortcut the trail. Desert vegetation, such as ocotillo, agave, creosote, and prickly pear, dominate the first two miles of trail.

Little shade exists.

Upon reaching the first bench at about 0.4 mile, the grade moderates somewhat. Sheer walls of limestone, dolomite, and sandstone tower 1,500 feet above the bench. Below the trail on the left, the creek tumbles down in a smaller inner canyon.

Views of White Sands open up to the west. The trail climbs steadily, reaching the second bench after about two miles.

The vegetation slowly changes. The level second bench is thickly covered with grasses, such as black gramma, sideoats gramma, and tobosa, and a few scattered alligator junipers.

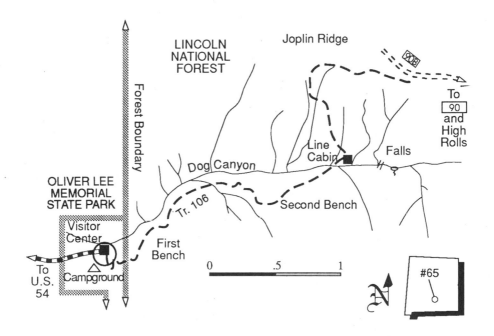

The bench makes one of the best camping areas on the hike.

The trail descends a short distance from the end of the bench to the lush riparian zone of the creek. The stream tumbles down cascades and into pools under the spreading branches of large cottonwoods and willows. A very rough half-mile bushwhack upstream leads the perseverant to a high waterfall pouring off the box at the head of the canyon. The old stone line cabin at the creek dates from the turn of the century.

Don't camp near the stream, the area is too small and delicate for such heavy use. Purify any water taken from the creek. At 2.4 miles and an elevation gain of 1,500 feet, the creek makes an excellent destination in itself.

The trail becomes very steep for the next 0.7 mile, gaining about 1000 feet as it climbs out of the canyon up the "Eyebrow." The views, especially at sunset, from the canyon rim are spectacular. Once out of the canyon, the trail climbs at a more moderate grade the last mile or so through pinon-juniper woodland to its end at FR 90B. The trail can be done as a one-way hike if a car shuttle is arranged in advance. A high-clearance vehicle is recommended for the forest road.

HIKE 66 *YUCCA CANYON*

General description: A moderate day hike or easy overnight trip into the Carlsbad Caverns Wilderness with views of rugged Slaughter Canyon.
General location: Carlsbad Caverns National Park.
Length: 5.5 miles round trip.
Elevation: 4,550-6,000 feet.
Maps: Grapevine Draw and Gunsight Canyon 7.5-minute USGS quads.
Best season: All year.
Water availability: Longview Spring, usually Dog Pen Seep.
Special attractions: Spectacular views; solitude
Permit: Required for camping; obtain at park headquarters.
Finding the trailhead: Follow the same directions as for Hike 67, Goat Cave. However, rather than following the directions all the way to the parking lot at the end of the road, stop about a mile short at the fenced and marked park boundary (where the pavement ends). Turn left (west) on the small dirt road that follows the fence line just inside the park. You will reach the Yucca Canyon parking lot in about two miles at the end of the road. A high clearance vehicle is preferable for this road, but, with care, a sedan can probably make it. Beware the shrubs that try to remove your vehicle's paint.

The hike: The Guadalupe Mountains form a very steep escarpment on the east flank that rises steadily to the south, reaching the highest point, 8,749 feet, in Guadalupe Mountains National Park. Carlsbad Caverns National Park follows the middle section of the escarpment, with escarpment elevations of about 4,000 feet in the northeast section of the park rising to 6,500 feet in the southwest section of the park. At the park visitor center the escarpment rises 800 feet above the valley floor. At Yucca Canyon the relief has increased to 2,000 feet.

Most visitors to the park only see the Chihuahuan desert at Carlsbad Caverns or New Cave. However, the higher southwestern end of the park adjoins Lincoln National Forest and is partially wooded with pinyon pine, alligator juniper, Gambel's oak, and even some ponderosa pine and bigtooth maple. Since almost no one hikes into the park's back country, you probably will have Yucca Canyon all to yourself.

From the parking lot, the trail follows the canyon bottom with a steady grade all the way to the top of the escarpment. The trail is generally in good condition and easy to follow. For the most part, the trail lies on the south side of the canyon bottom, but occasionally crosses to the north side. As you climb higher, a few junipers and madrones begin to appear, cacti start to give way to grasses.

The trail reaches the top abruptly, giving dramatic views northeast and southwest of the Guadalupe Mountains' steep escarpment. The trail runs into a large fenced study enclosure, built to study plant growth without deer browsing.

Follow the trail along the south fence of the enclosure to the west corner. Turn right at the corner and follow the trail along the west fence of the enclosure to the park service patrol cabin. The cabin is about two miles from the trailhead. The faint cairn-marked trail leading west from the fenced enclosure's west corner is a long, but scenic, route up into the Lincoln National Forest.

Near the park service cabin are the ruins of an older cabin. Gnarled alligator juniper, smooth reddish-barked madrones, and stunted pinyon pines grow in contrast to the desert below. Even a few scattered ponderosa pines eke out a living on the relatively level escarpment crest.

The trail to Longview Spring, marked by rock cairns, runs west from the old cabin. The trail slowly curves right as it drops into a shallow grassy draw. The old walls of a corral mark Dog Pen Seep. Just beyond the walls, on the north side of the draw, water drips over a ledge. Except in dry years, water is usually available here.

The trail continues past the seep down the draw. As the draw gets deeper, the trail moves onto a wide ledge on the south side above the bottom. Soon you reach the mouth of the draw, where it joins a much larger and deeper canyon. Continue to follow the trail along the ledge as it turns left. Some rusted farm implements signal that the spring is just ahead in a lush green patch of vegetation. Cool water trickles out of a broken pipe and from another terrace below. Longview Spring is nearly always reliable, but in especially dry years ask at park headquarters for an update on its condition.

From the spring, the heart of the Carlsbad Caverns Wilderness is spread out before you. The broad ledges of the spring look out on an incredible view of rugged West Slaughter Canyon over 1,000 feet below. The sheer cliffs and steep slopes look virtually impassable. Ponderosa pines and bigtooth maples cling to ledges on the moister north-facing slopes underneath you.

If you camp, be sure to obtain a permit at park headquarters beforehand. The areas near the two springs and the patchy woodland around the cabin have many ideal campsites. So that wildlife may drink, be sure not to camp any closer than at least 100 yards from the springs. Ground fires are not permitted in the park.

The hike can be easily done in a day, but plan to stay overnight to allow time to explore the ridgetops overlooking the escarpment and the canyons. Get an early start in summer since it can be hot. Occasional snow storms blow through in winter and spring can be windy, but the hike is appropriate all year.

HIKE 67 *GOAT CAVE*

General description: A moderate hike to a large cave in the Carlsbad Caverns Wilderness.
General location: Carlsbad Caverns National Park.
Length: Six miles round trip.
Elevation: 4,200-4700 feet.
Maps:. Serpentine Bends and Grapevine Draw 7.5- minute USGS quads.
Best season: Fall through spring.
Water availability: None.
Special attractions: A large limestone cave; solitude.
Permit: The National Park Service requires a permit for entry into the cave itself. Obtain at park headquarters.
Finding the trailhead: Drive five miles south of White's City (twenty-five miles south of Carlsbad) on US 62-180 to the paved turnoff marked by the Park Service as the route to New Cave. Turn and follow the Park Service signs eleven more miles to the New Cave parking lot in the wide mouth of Slaughter Canyon.

The hike: The Guadalupe Mountains of New Mexico and Texas form one of three exposures of the fossilized Capitan Reef, the world's largest. The other two exposures, also uplifted by faults, are the Apache and Glass Mountains far to the south in West Texas. Slaughter Canyon is the largest drainage contained largely within Carlsbad Caverns National Park. Its rugged defile cuts a 1,400-foot deep gash in the mountains.

Much of the Guadalupe Mountains' fame comes from the massive limestone caves, especially Carlsbad Caverns. The Capitan Reef formed as an homogenous mass, rather than in thin layers, allowing the formation of enormous rooms and passages. Thin layers do not have sufficient structural strength to form large roof spans. For years, scientists believed that the Guadalupe caves were formed, as in most areas, by the dissolving action of carbon dioxide dissolved in rainwater (carbonic acid). Recent research, however, indicates that some of the large caves formed instead by the dissolving action of sulfuric acid, created from hydrogen sulfide gas. The gas, which also gives rotten eggs their smell, comes from the natural seepage of oil and gas reservoirs, common in the area.

From the parking lot, follow the signs marked "Middle Slaughter Canyon" up the bottom of the canyon. Don't take the New Cave trail. For the first few hundred yards, the trail follows the dry white cobble bottom of the broad canyon floor. Follow the rock cairns when the trail isn't obvious. It soon climbs up the left bank onto the remains of an old road. The trail follows the old road for about one-half mile.

Chihuahuan Desert vegetation dominates the hike, with lechuguilla, sotol, cholla, and other desert plants common. You are unlikely to see anyone else on your hike.

Just after the old road reenters the broad canyon wash, a very large tributary, West Slaughter Canyon, joins the main canyon from the left. Continue to follow the rock cairns into the north fork of the canyon, rather than turning left into

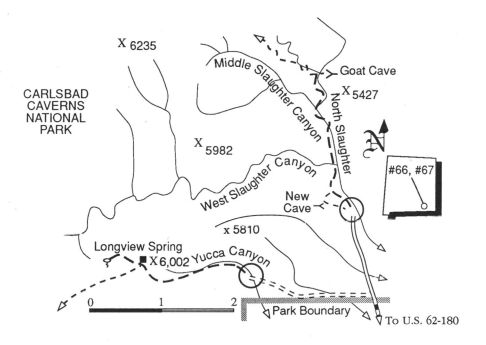

the west fork. After several hundred yards of crossing the white cobble bottom, the trail climbs back onto a low bench on the left, or west, side of North Slaughter Canyon. About one-half mile farther, the trail again crosses the canyon floor to the site of an old homestead on a grassy bench on the east side. Not much more than a few corral posts and rusty tin cans remain.

Continue up the canyon back into the dry wash bottom. A short distance up the wash, the canyon forks again. Take the right fork into North Slaughter Canyon, following the cairns. Right after the fork, the trail climbs up onto the lefthand bench for a short distance, but drops back into the wash again. The trail sometimes climbs back up onto the benches, but, because the north fork is much narrower and windier, much of the rest of the route stays in the wash bottom. In the narrower canyon, you will begin to see a few oak trees and even an occasional bigtooth maple. The higher and lusher McKittrick Canyon to the south in Guadalupe Mountains National Park is famous for the brilliant fall color of its many maples.

At the next canyon junction, the trail will be on the lefthand, or west bench, as it turns into the left canyon fork. Leave the trail at the junction and reenter the rocky wash. The Goat Cave entrance lies at the base of the huge limestone fin above the righthand, or east, bench of the canyon. Look carefully along the side of the east bench at the canyon fork for a steep rocky trail leading up to the base of the rock fin. Beware the catclaw shrubs trying to grab your clothes and exposed flesh as you scramble up a couple hundred feet to the cave mouth. The entrance, although huge, is not visible from the canyon bottom at the fork since it faces up canyon. If you have trouble finding the trail to the cave, walk up the right canyon fork a couple hundred yards until you can see the cave entrance.

To enter the cave, you must have obtained a permit from the park service. The cave is not heavily decorated, but is impressive because of its size. It consists of a long straight passage over 0.25 mile long. Light shines down from a window high in the ceiling. With only one short side passage, you can't get lost, but be sure that each member of your group takes three sources of light and wears a hard hat. Don't enter the cave alone. Walk lightly in the entrance; it's very dusty.

The return trip follows the same route. Particularly in the wide lower part of the canyon, it's possible to shorten the hike slightly by walking straight down the wash bottom, rather than following the trail on the low benches. However, the benches are much easier to walk on than the rocky, cobbly wash and thus are quicker. The hike can be done in summer, but is very hot, with little shade. Occasional snow storms quickly blow through in winter and spring can be windy, making fall the best season for the hike.

HIKE 68 *SITTING BULL FALLS*

General description: An easy day hike to one of the few flowing streams in the Guadalupe Mountains.
General location: About forty-five miles southwest of Carlsbad.
Length: One-half mile round trip to falls; 2.5 miles round trip to spring.
Elevation: 4,650-5,000 feet.
Maps: Lincoln National Forest (Guadalupe District), Red Bluff Draw and Queen 7.5-minute USGS quads.
Best season: All year.
Water availability: Trailhead, Sitting Bull Creek.
Special attractions: One of the largest waterfalls in New Mexico.
Finding the trailhead: Drive twelve miles north from Carlsbad on US 285 to the junction of NM 137. Turn and follow 137 about twenty-five miles southwest to the marked turnoff (Forest Road 276) to Sitting Bull Falls. Drive eight miles to the parking lot at the end of the road. The falls are well known and are even shown on many state highway maps.

The hike: Depending on rainfall, you may drive across the running stream a couple of times before you reach the parking lot. A large developed picnic area, with restrooms and running water, flanks the parking area. The area is very popular and crowded on summer and holiday weekends. Try to visit on weekdays, ideally before Memorial Day or after Labor Day. Although the trails follow the stream, the area receives heavy use, making water purification very necessary. Carry water from the picnic ground taps, even though its taste leaves something to be desired.

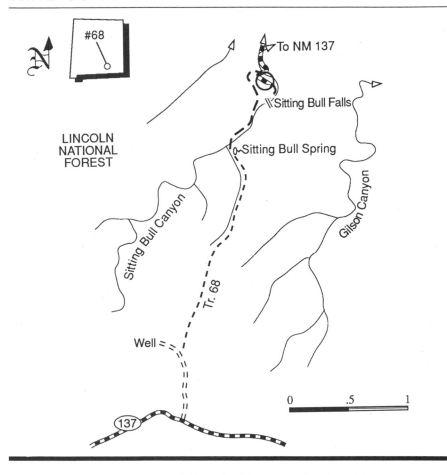

The water of the 130-foot falls is highly mineralized and has deposited a massive travertine bluff that towers over the picnic ground. The size of the travertine deposit indicates that the falls may have been much bigger in times past.

The hike is split into two parts. Follow the trail southeast through the picnic area a few hundred yards to the falls. The falls pour off of an overhanging travertine bluff high above in a sparkling quicksilver shower. People often swim in the pools at the base of the falls. The permanent water in the dry semi-desert foothills of the Guadalupe Mountains creates an oasis of ash, sawgrass, walnut, chinkapin oak, madrone, and even ponderosa pine. Maidenhair ferns cling to crevices in the wet travertine and flowers are abundant.

The area has received considerable damage from heavy visitation. Try to avoid additional damage by staying on the trail and off of the delicate vegetation. Even with the heavy use, however, the falls and stream are very beautiful and unlike any other area in New Mexico.

To reach Sitting Bull Spring, take the marked trail (68) from the opposite side of the parking area as the falls trail. The trail quickly climbs the 200 feet up to the small plateau at the top of the falls. The trail reaches the creek in about one-half mile. A short side trip downstream to the top of the falls is worthwhile. The creek flows through several deep pools before reaching the falls. Again, please be careful not to damage the delicate vegetation and travertine. The area is already heavily trampled and criss-crossed by trails. Be careful at the top of the falls; people have died by falling off the slippery cliff.

Upstream, the trail continues for another three-quarters of a mile to the spring, enclosed by the Forest Service. Along the way you will pass more lush riparian vegetation and a rushing stream with many deep pools. The trail can be followed for about another 2.5 miles past the spring to the continuation of NM 137, but the most scenic part is between the spring and the falls. One reward for going further, however, will be the lack of people. Less than a mile beyond the spring, the trail climbs out onto the canyon rim, giving good views of the surrounding country.

The Forest Service doesn't allow camping at the falls or picnic area, but does allow it above the falls. Try to resist the temptation to camp along the heavily used stream area and set up camp well away from the watercourse.

HIKE 69 *BIG CANYON*

General description: An easy day hike onto a promontory overlooking the fork between the three main branches of Big Canyon.
General location: About sixty-five miles southwest of Carlsbad.
Length: About four miles round trip.
Elevation: 7,220-6,800 ft.
Maps: Lincoln National Forest/Guadalupe District, Guadalupe Mountains National Park trails illustrated topo map, El Paso Gap 7.5-minute USGS quad.
Best season: Year round.
Water availability: None.
Special attractions: Tremendous views of rugged country.
Finding the trailhead: Drive about twelve miles northwest of Carlsbad on US 285 to the NM 137 junction. Turn left (southwest) and follow paved NM 137 about 41.5 miles to the well-marked junction with Forest Road 540, the Guadalupe Ridge Road. Turn left onto the good gravel road FR 540 and follow it just over twelve miles to the end of the improved gravel surface in a parking area. Two dirt roads depart from the parking lot. Follow the better road to the right (south), marked with a Guadalupe Ridge Trail 201 sign. Ignore the bad road forking to the right at 0.3 mile and drive 0.8 mile further to a fork on the top of a ridge. The fork, marked as an unmaintained primitive road, is the trail. With care, any vehicle should be able to make the last rough 1.1 miles to the fork without any problem.

The hike: The trail ends on a point overlooking one of the deepest and most rugged canyons in the Guadalupe Mountains. The canyon cuts through 1,800 feet of rock at the mouth, including the fossil Capitan Reef. The limestone reef, largest in the world, contains many caves, including the famous Carlsbad

Vultures roost before an impending thunderstorm in the Guadalupe Mountains near Big Canyon.

Caverns. The trail follows a wooded ridge with only slight ups and downs along the way.

The trail is good any time of year. Snow falls occasionally in winter, but melts quickly. Spring is probably the least desirable season, with frequent heavy winds.

The trail starts east along the primitive road in a forest of alligator juniper, pinon pine, and stunted ponderosa pine. Here and there views open up to the north and south into different forks of Big Canyon. Although there is considerable ponderosa pine on the tops of the Guadalupe Mountains, most of it is stunted by the marginal rainfall. In more sheltered canyons and slopes, the ponderosas thrive, along with scattered Douglas fir and even a few aspen.

The first half mile or so can be driven by four-wheel drive vehicles, but is very rocky. The primitive road formally ends at a parking area overlooking a southern view into a fork of Big Canyon. Unfortunately, since I first started going there, off-road vehicles have beaten in a rough road for most of the rest of the hike on what used to be the trail. Resist the impulse to drive it yourself. The road has destroyed much of the trees and vegetation and even runs directly over an archaeological site. The Forest Service has not tried to stop the use of the road. Write them and complain.

Even with the road, the hike is still spectacular. Continue down the road through the woods. At about 1.5 miles the road peters out above a beautiful sunken valley cut into the rim of the main canyon below. With a grassy bottom and scattered ponderosa pines, the sheltered valley makes an ideal camping spot. The small narrow valley, with its twenty-foot walls, was probably created when an large, long cave collapsed. The floor of Big Canyon lies 1,800 precipitous feet below. Follow a faint trail another 0.5 mile east out to a prominent point overlooking the fork between the three main branches of the canyon. The view, especially at sunrise or sunset, is hard to beat.

Since I last made this hike, a forest fire burned a large part of the Guadalupes in the summer of 1990. The fire may have affected part of this hike, but even if it did, the views are still worth the trip.

HIKE 70 *CAMP WILDERNESS RIDGE*

General description: A strenuous, but spectacular, overnight hike from Texas into New Mexico.
General location: About fifty-five miles southwest of Carlsbad.
Length: About fifteen miles round trip.
Elevation: 5,000-7,410 feet.
Maps: Guadalupe Mountains National Park trails illustrated topo map, Lincoln National Forest—Guadalupe District, El Paso Gap, Guadalupe Peak, and Independence Spring 7.5-minute USGS quads.
Best season: Year round.
Water availability: Trailhead.
Special attractions: Rugged canyons, views.
Permit: Required for overnight camping; obtain at Guadalupe Mountains National Park visitor center.
Finding the trailhead: Drive south from Carlsbad on US 62-180 into Texas to the Guadalupe Mountains National Park— McKittrick Canyon turnoff. Turn right onto the paved, well-marked road and follow it about 4.5 miles to the parking lot and information station at the end of the road.

The hike: The trail starts in the mouth of McKittrick Canyon at the Park Service information station. From there, the trail climbs up the north wall of the canyon and crosses into the Lincoln National Forest of New Mexico. McKittrick Canyon is famous for it permanent stream and fall display of bigtooth maples. Be sure to fill up water bottles at the information station, since there is no water on the canyon rim.

From the information station, follow the signs for the Permian Reef Geology Trail, rather than those pointing up the canyon. The trail quickly crosses the broad dry wash of the canyon and begins climbing up a bench on the other side. With a series of large switchbacks, the trail steadily climbs the 2,000 feet up to the canyon rim. The trail climbs the south-facing wall of the canyon and is hot in summer. Because of the solar exposure, desert vegetation dominates until the trail reaches the rim at about 7000 feet.

As the trail climbs, it crosses the limestone heart of the ancient Capitan Reef. Fossils abound in the broken rock along the trail, but since this is a national park be sure to leave them in place. The trail is a favorite of geology students from much of the Southwest.

Upon reaching the rim at about 3.5 miles, the trail abruptly levels out. Tremendous views open up of the rugged McKittrick watershed and of the plains stretching endlessly to the southeast. The rest of the trail consists of only mild ups and downs as it follows the rim of North McKittrick Canyon into New Mexico. The vegetation changes radically at the rim, from prickly pear, sotol, catclaw, and other desert plants to grassy meadows with pinon, ponderosa, and alligator juniper.

A little more than 0.5 mile from the rim, the trail reaches the designated Park Service campsite. To camp here you need to have obtained a permit from the Park Service. A short distance further, in the Lincoln National Forest, no permit is necessary. However, if you plan to leave your vehicle overnight in

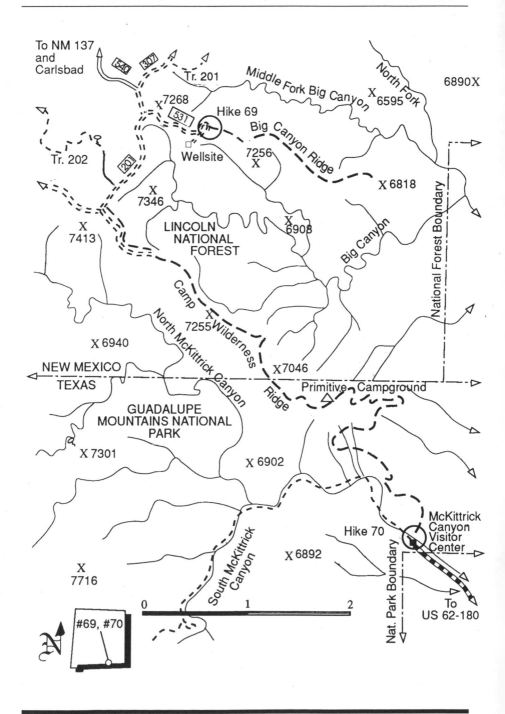

the McKittrick Canyon parking lot, you must inform the Park Service beforehand, since they lock the gate at the highway at night.

About 0.6 mile past the Park Service campsite, the trail crosses a fence into the Lincoln National Forest of New Mexico. The trail follows the canyon rim northwest for about 1.25 miles from the state line, where the trail turns into an extremely rough four-wheel drive road. Continue along the road for another 1.6 miles to the end of this hike. At this point the road turns north and leaves the canyon rim.

About fifty yards down from the rim, the road splits. The left fork continues across the mountain top for a short distance before turning into a trail. The right fork leads to another access point as described below.

Taking the trail just up to the rim and back makes a good, although strenuous dayhike. To halve the hike, a car shuttle is possible. Follow the directions for finding the Big Canyon hike (69) trailhead. Instead of going 1.1 miles from the gravel parking lot described, go only 0.3 mile to the "bad road" described as forking off to the right. Unless you have a four-wheel drive vehicle, park at the fork and walk 1.1 miles along the "bad road" to the junction at the canyon rim described in the paragraph above. Ignore the right fork (Forest Road 202) encountered at 0.8 mile. Even with a four-wheel drive, the road is extremely rocky and difficult to drive on. The stretch of road along the canyon rim becomes almost impassable. Walking is recommended. The hike is much easier to do in reverse, if you have a car shuttle waiting at the McKittrick Canyon parking lot.

Anytime of year is good for hiking in the Guadalupes. Be prepared for occasional snows in winter and thunderstorms in late summer. The Guadalupes are notorious for their winds in spring. I've nearly been blown off the tops of the mountains in April. Fall is probably the ideal season, although the bottom of McKittrick Canyon is very busy on fall color weekends in late October.

ADDITIONAL INFORMATION

Government Agencies

Bandelier National Monument, HCR 1, Box 1, Ste. 15, Los Alamos, NM 87544 (505) 672-3861

Bureau of Land Management, 1235 La Plata Highway Farmington, NM 87401 (505) 327-5344

1800 Marquess St., Las Cruces, NM 88005 (505) 525-8228

204 Cruz Alta, Taos, NM 87571-6168 (505) 758-8851

Capulin Volcano National Monument, Capulin, NM 88414 (505) 278-2201

Carlsbad Caverns National Park, 3225 National Parks Highway, Carlsbad, NM 88220 (505) 785-2233

Carson National Forest—Headquarters, P.O. Box 558, Taos, NM 87571 (505) 758-6200

Camino Real Ranger District, P.O. Box 68, Penasco, NM 87553 (505) 587-2255

Questa Ranger District, P.O. Box 110 Questa, NM 87556 (505) 586-0520

Chaco Culture National Historical Park, Star Route 4, Box 6500, Bloomfield, NM 87413 (505) 988-6716

Cibola National Forest—Headquarters, 2113 Osuna Road NE, Ste. A, Albuquerque, NM 87112 (505)761-4650

Magdalena Ranger District, P.O. Box 45, Magdalena, NM 87825 (505) 854-2381

Mountainair Ranger District, P.O. Box E, Mountainair, NM 87036 (505) 847-2990

Mount Taylor Ranger District, 1800 Lobo Canyon Road, Grants, NM 87020 (505) 287-8833

Sandia Ranger District, 11776 Highway 337, Tijeras, NM 87059 (505) 281-3304

Coronado National Forest—Headquarters, 300 W. Congress, Tucson, AZ 85701 (602) 670-6483

Douglas Ranger District, RR 1, Box 228R, Douglas, AZ 85607 (602) 364-3468

El Malpais National Monument, 620 E. Santa Fe Street, Grants, NM 87020 (505) 285-4641

Gila Cliff Dwellings National Monument, Gila National Forest, Wilderness District, Route 11, Box 100, Silver City, NM 88061 (505) 536-9461

Gila National Forest—Headquarters, 2610 N. Silver St., Silver City, NM 88061 (505) 388-8201

Black Range Ranger District, P.O. Box 431, Truth or Consequences, NM 87901 (505) 894-6677

Glenwood Ranger District, Box 8, Glenwood, NM 88039 (505) 539-2281

Mimbres Ranger District, Box 79, Mimbres, NM 88049 (505) 536-2250

Reserve Ranger District, P.O. Box 117, Reserve, NM 87830 (505) 533-6231

Silver City Ranger District, 2915 Highway 180, East Silver City, NM 88061 (505) 538-2771

Guadalupe Mountains National Park, HC 60, Box 400, Salt Flat, TX 79847 (915) 828-3251

Lincoln National Forest—Headquarters, Federal Building, 11th and New York, Alamogordo, NM 88310 (505) 437-6030

Lincoln National Forest, Cloudcroft Ranger District, P.O. Box 288, Cloudcroft, NM 88317 (505) 682-2551

Lincoln National Forest, Guadalupe Ranger District, Federal Building, Rm. 159, Carlsbad, NM 88220 (505) 885-4181

Lincoln National Forest, Smokey Bear Ranger District, 901 Mechem Dr., Ruidoso, NM 88345 (505) 257-4095

Santa Fe National Forest—Headquarters, P.O. Box 1689, Santa Fe, NM 87504 (505) 988-6940

Coyote Ranger District, P.O. Box 160, Coyote, NM 87012 (505) 638-5526

Cuba Ranger District, P.O. Box 130, Cuba, NM 87013 (505) 289-3264

Espanola Ranger District, P.O. Box R, Espanola, NM 87532 (505) 753-7331

Jemez Ranger District, Jemez Springs, NM 87025 (505) 829-3535

Las Vegas Office, 1926 N. 7th St., Las Vegas, NM 87701 (505) 425-3534

Los Alamos Office, 528 35th St., Los Alamos, NM 87544 (505) 667-5120

Pecos-Las Vegas Ranger District, P.O. Drawer 429, Pecos, NM 87552 (505) 757-6121

U.S. Geological Survey, ESIC-Denver, 169 Federal Building, 1961 Stout St., Denver, CO 80294 (303) 844-4169

White Sands National Monument, P.O. Box 458, Alamogordo, NM 88310 (505) 479-6124

ADDITIONAL READING

Day Hikes In The Santa Fe Area. The Santa Fe Group of the Sierra Club, Santa Fe, NM, Third Edition 1990.

Evans, Harry. *50 Hikes In New Mexico.* Gem Guides Book Company, Pico Rivera, CA, 1984, revised 1988.

Ganci, Dave. *Hiking The Southwest: Arizona, New Mexico, and West Texas.* Sierra Club Books, San Francisco, CA, 1983.

Hill, Mike. *Hikers and Climbers Guide To The Sandias.* University of New Mexico Press, Albuquerque, NM, 1983.

Hoard, Dorothy. *A Guide To Bandelier National Monument.* Los Alamos Historical Society, Los Alamos, NM, 1989.

Magee, Greg S. *'El Paisaje De Soledad' The Land Scape of Solitude: A Hiking Guide To Dona Ana County, New Mexico.* Roseta Press, Las Cruces, NM, 1989.

Matthews, Kay. *Hiking Trails of the Sandia and Manzano Mountains.* Heritage Association, Inc., Albuquerque, New Mexico, 1984.

McDonald, Corry. *Wilderness: A New Mexico Legacy.* Sunstone Press, Santa Fe, NM, 1985.

Murray, John A. *The Gila Wilderness: A Hiking Guide.* University of New Mexico Press, Albuquerque, NM, 1988.

Overhage, Carl. *One Day Walks In The Pecos Wilderness.* Sunstone Press, Santa Fe, NM, 1980, revised 1984.

Perry, John and Jane Greverus. *The Sierra Club Guide To The Natural Areas of New Mexico, Arizona, and Nevada.* Sierra Club Books, San Francisco, CA, 1985.

Ungnade, Herbert E. *Guide To The New Mexico Mountains.* University of New Mexico Press, Albuquerque, NM, 1965.

ABOUT THE AUTHOR

Laurence and Patricia Parent.

Laurence Parent was born and raised in New Mexico. After receiving an engineering degree at the University of Texas at Austin, he practiced engineering for six years before becoming a full-time freelance photographer and writer specializing in landscape, travel, and nature subjects. His photos appear in Sierra Club, Audubon, and many other calendars. His article and photo credits include *National Geographic Traveler, Outside, Backpacker, Sierra,* and the *New York Times.* He contributes regularly to regional publications such as *Texas Highways, Texas Monthly, New Mexico Magazine,* and *Texas Parks & Wildlife.* Other work includes posters, advertising, museum exhibits, postcards, and brochures.

He has completed several books, including one for Falcon Press, "The Hiker's Guide to Texas." His work also appears in Falcon's "New Mexico on My Mind" and "Texas on My Mind" books, Falcon Press calendars, and other Falcon products. He makes his home in Austin, Texas with his wife patricia.

Out here—there's no one to ask directions

...except your **FALCON**GUIDE.

FALCONGUIDES is a series of recreation guidebooks designed to help you safely enjoy the great outdoors. Each title features up-to-date maps, photos, and detailed information on access, hazards, side trips, special attractions, and more. The 6 x 9" softcover format makes every book an ideal companion as you discover the scenic wonders around you.

FALCONGUIDES...lead the way!